On an Open Fire

Roasting · Barbecuing · Cooking

CARSTEN BOTHE

On an Open Fire

Roasting · Barbecuing · Cooking

4880 Lower Valley Road • Atglen, PA 19310

Designed by Molly Shields
Type set in DIN-BoldAlternate/DIN-RegularAlternate
ISBN: by 978-0-7643-4483-1
Printed in China

Originally published as Auf Offenem Feuer Grillen, Braten, Kochen by DSR Werbeagentur Rypka GmbH, Graz
© 2011 by Leopold Socker Verlag, Graz (ISBN: 978-3-7020-1297-7)
Translated from the German by Omicron Language Solutions, LLC

Published by Schiffer Publishing, Ltd.
4880 Lower Valley Road
Atglen, PA 19310
Phone: (610) 593-1777; Fax: (610) 593-2002
E-mail: Info@schifferbooks.com

For our complete selection of fine books on this and related subjects, please visit our website at www.schifferbooks.com. You may also write for a free catalog.

This book may be purchased from the publisher. Please try your bookstore first.

We are always looking for people to write books on new and related subjects. If you have an idea for a book, please contact us at proposals@schifferbooks.com.

Schiffer Publishing's titles are available at special discounts for bulk purchases for sales promotions or premiums. Special editions, including personalized covers, corporate imprints, and excerpts can be created in large quantities for special needs. For more information, contact the publisher.

Contents

CONTENTS

FOREWORD

Dear reader,

The camp fire has had a unique fascination for millennia. It promises warmth, comfort, safety, nourishment. Who doesn't know the feeling of looking into the camp fire for hours and smelling the aroma of the fire, hearing the crackling of the wood as it burns, and feeling the warmth of the flames. If there is a delicious roast turning in front of the fire, and potatoes and onions baking in the embers, and hot coffee waiting in a pot, then you really have it made.

For centuries, if not millennia, humans have prepared their food by the open fire, completely without a ceramic glass cooktop and microwave. It still works as well today as it did back then—and as it still does in a large part of the world. A large number of dishes can be prepared surprisingly fast and easily by the open fire, and in large quantities to boot. Barbecuing is only one of the preparation methods. The many types of preparation range from roasting on a stick or a rope and cooking in the embers to cooking in a fire pit. And each one has its own appeal and advantages.

Dear reader, feel free to try the many possibilities and variations of preparation by the open fire. It is simply fun to try something new, instead of always grilling sausages. Cooking by the fire is more than just preparing food. it lets us be one with our past.

I wish you good luck and enjoy your meal!

CARSTEN BOTHE

SETTING UP A CAMPFIRE KITCHEN

Peculiarities of a Campfire Kitchen

Cooking outdoors today usually means barbecuing. When barbecuing is a cozy get-together, the kitchen, with its electric appliances, isn't far away. Meat and vegetables come straight from the refrigerator.

Cooking outdoors, whether it's on a longer hike in an inhospitable terrain or simply because it's fun and tastes good, goes far beyond barbecuing. It is a step back into the wild romance of the past, as trappers, soldiers, or tradesmen indulged in a freshly prepared meal; this was a treat for them because, as a rule, their food consisted of dried, smoked, or corned meat. Only food that couldn't spoil—for example, corned pork that was covered with lard in barrels—was suitable for the vagabond life of the cowboys or soldiers. However, in between there was fresh meat, and that was—just like the other food—prepared by the campfire.

Even though you can prepare multicourse meals by the campfire, typical fare will be limited to single-pot dishes and occasionally something roasted with a side dish. Accordingly, you can get by with a pot and a pan. A tripod is a necessary accessory to be able to place the pot or pan over the fire. Also, you will need a bowl to prepare the food, knead the dough, and wash the dishes afterward. A wooden board is handy for cutting. It should be fairly large but but not too thick, so it weighs less.

You should procure a cooking trunk for transporting your utensils, because its lid can serve for sitting or as a table, and it offers added space for setting things down.

A proper cooking trunk serves as a table too.

The Most Important Items: Wood and Charcoal

Without fuel the campfire kitchen won't work. The campfire has three zones: the flame, the embers, and the ashes. All three zones are needed for the various types of food preparation. So, if you should desire to cook on an open fire, you must not remove the ashes from it, because you can cook fabulously in them. They are also needed as an insulation layer against too much heat from the fire.

The best wood to use is dry, healthy hardwood such as beech or oak, untreated and cut into pieces the thickness of an arm. Since space at the campfire—if you use it for cooking—is always very tight, logs that are ten to twelve inches long are most practical. With this wood you produce the needed embers for grilling or cooking.

To get sufficient embers from a fire, ten to twelve of these wood pieces should burn for about two hours. Then, you remove the still smoking pieces from the ember pile with tongs and place them together, so that a flame starts up again. It is easiest to prevent the pieces from smoking by coaxing them back into a flame. The smoke disappears instantly. A good fire burns without smoke and fumes.

Sufficient embers are only produced by a fire that has been burning for a few hours. Therefore, a fire from the previous evening is ideal. The subsoil of the fire pit should consist of loose sand, because then the ashes mix with the sand and provide even better insulation.

To cook over the fire—if you need a very hot fire pit quickly—use wood the thickness of your thumb exclusively. It will catch fire quickly and burn with a hot flame, which will quickly heat up the pot or pan. The disadvantage is that the pots are quickly spoiled by the soot, so you should stay away from this type of firing if possible.

Aside from wood, charcoal and the charcoal briquettes made from it are well suited for a cooking fire. However, there are huge differences in quality and you should not use the worst quality. This charcoal or the charcoal briquettes smoke and leave behind cinders of stone and pieces of uncharred wood.

This amount of wood, about 2.5 pounds or 1 kilogram, the thickness of a thumb has the effect of a cooktop with 15 kW/h.

Fixed Fire Pit

Cooking by a campfire is an incredibly strenuous task. You don't really notice it until you have moved a few heavy pans or a Dutch oven by the fire. For some inexplicable reasons all people build their first fire pit the same way: dig a hole and place rocks around it. That means that you have to bend down even further to cook. You stand less securely, and inevitably the contents of your shirt and apron pockets falls into the fire. It is better to place rocks in a circle and to fill the interior with fine sand to raise the fire. The shape of a keyhole is also well suited for cooking: the fire is kept in the large part to produce embers. Then the embers are scraped into the elongated part for cooking.

If you enjoy cooking in the garden or at the hunting cabin, or do it often, you should set up an elevated fireplace. It does not need to be built out of bricks; loose rocks stacked on top of solid ground are completely sufficient. The important part is the backdrop of stacked rocks, which allows you to create several heat zones even on a small surface area. The fireplace depicted on p. 14, top left, consists of a core of old Ytong cinder blocks covered with simple floor tiles.

An elevated fireplace built of old stones

An improvised, elongated cooking place: In the back portion the embers are produced; in the front you cook in Dutch ovens.

Here are the five zones of campfire cuisine:
1 = Fire to produce embers; 2 = Embers for grilling or for baked potatoes; 3 = Cooking with the Dutch oven
4 = Coffee pot; 5 = Table surface for preparations.

A grill like this allows you to cook with the fire at a comfortable height.

It is practical to pound two of the bars into the ground and place the third one across them.

Short Anecdote:

I was supposed to cook for friends by the campfire and had ordered a fire that was supposed to have burned for two hours before I arrived, so there would be embers. What I found was a hole, three feet in diameter, twenty inches deep, filled with embers. It looked as if you had kicked open the door to hell. You couldn't stay next to the pit for more than a few seconds, let alone think of cooking; it would have been better for casting bronze. My friends were quite surprised that I only needed a small shovel of embers for each of the Dutch ovens.

The upper parts of the rods consist of two closed and one open loop, which makes it easy to combine them into a tripod.

Rods

For a campfire, typically, two rods are pounded into the ground and are connected with a third one. This type of attachment has a decisive advantage over the usual tripod: you can only attach one pot to a tripod and you cannot push it away from the fire easily. The advantage of the tripod is: it is a bit more stable and is, of course, the top choice for holding a single heavy pot over the fire.

The rods for the fire are manufactured by any local blacksmith at little cost. Good measurements for the rods are:

• Length: 75 inches (190 cm)
• Rod diameter: 1/2 inch (14 mm)
• Interior diameter of the eyelet 2-1/4 inches (60 mm)

The rods should not be significantly shorter, and, especially, not any thinner, since they will not be able to support the weight of the pots otherwise.

In addition, thin material bends when you pound it into the ground or the eyelets squeeze shut when you hit them with the hammer.

A pan support is necessary for cooking by the fire.

> **Tip:**
>
> Purchase ladles (scoops) and other kitchen tools with a hook instead of an eyelet at the end. This way you can easily hang the items on the rod. They will also not slide into the pot.

Poker

Owning a nice poker is a good thing. Even though tongs are considerably more handy, it is indescribably pleasant to poke in the fire with a poker in the evening, drink a glass of grog, and talk with good friends about God and the world. In earlier times the heated poker was used to reheat cold beverages which developed into the German custom of Bierstachelns (poking beer).

In earlier times, beer was consumed warm. For this, an iron—the Bierstachel (beer poker)—was heated in the fire and dipped into the drink. Aside from the heating, the sugar is caramelized leading to better taste.

Trivet

To place pans or pots without attached feet over the embers, a trivet is necessary. If you spend much time cooking on soft ground, you should get one with curved feet, so the support area is larger. This is not necessary in a brick cooking area. Don't let yourself be fooled with the height: One width of the hand is just right.

Field Grill

If you want to get more intensely into cooking at the campfire, you won't be able to avoid a field cooking grill. Even Roman legionnaires used these.

A field cook stove is meant for more intense use.

The top side has a surface area of about 24 inches square (60 x 60 cm), as large as a standard ceramic glass cooktop. On such a field grill you can prepare quite a bit of food.

Rocks

You can easily build a fire pit with rocks. Bricks are ideal, however, since they are evenly sized. You can use rocks to support a pan or a pot over the embers, or an improvised grill. Skewers with meat can rest on the rocks with both ends supported. When roasting on a rotisserie, you can protect the frying pan (which catches the dripping fat) placed underneath it from too much radiated heat using bricks standing upright.

Coffee Pot

Coffee pot specifically for use at the campfire

For heating water and making coffee there are two pot shapes. A tall coffee pot is placed by the fire with the spout pointing at the fire. It heats up from the radiating warmth, and the handle remains relatively cold. The teapot, with the flatter shape and the handle attached to the top, has to be placed on top of the fire or suspended above it.

Pan

A pan for use on the open fire has different requirements for its material and design than a pan meant for use on the electric cooktop. For one thing it must not have any plastic parts on the handle. The nonstick treatments also handle overheating very poorly, which can happen fairly quickly on the open fire. Aluminum is eliminated from consideration completely since it can melt in the fire. That only leaves wrought iron or cast iron. Wrought iron is a good and affordable solution for a small frying pan. If you need a larger model though, you won't be able to avoid cast iron. Cast iron keeps its shape even with uneven heat, which is not true for thinner metal. In metal pans the bottom tends to warp and the fat collects in a low spot while the meat burns at another place. Cast iron has another advantage since, due to its great mass, a cast iron pan absorbs the heat and distributes it evenly. For browning steaks the cast iron frying pan also does not lose its temperature as quickly when placing the cold meat into it, which is where the good roasting characteristics come from.

Cast iron pan on a trivet

The wrought iron pans have to be conditioned first. Here, in addition to the oven method, you also have the option to pretreat the pan on the cooktop. First, clean the pan and set it on the cooktop. Put a bit of fat into the pan and place raw potato slices so that they tightly touch each other. The slices should be one centimeter thick and lie flat. The potato is only meant to keep from heating the pan empty, so it does not need to be peeled. As soon as the potato slices are almost black, throw them away, let the pan cool down, and wipe the fat off with a paper towel. That's it! Now you can use the pan for frying. It will keep getting better. Do not wash out the pan with dish washing detergent under any circumstances. Wiping it out with a kitchen towel is typically enough.

This pan is wrought from a single piece and is also a top product for use at the campfire, especially due to the long handle.

Gloves

You should always have a pair of heat-resistant gloves (welder's gloves from the home improvement store, baking gloves from the bakery) ready by the fire, in case you have to rescue something from it. The trick when cooking by the open fire is exactly that, being able to do everything by hand. However, gloves hide a particular danger if they burn, since you won't notice it until it is too late, because the insulation does its job even in this case.

Such a glove is also very dangerous with wet heat. If boiling water is poured over it, it absorbs the hot liquid and burns your hand if you can't take off the glove fast enough.

Look for long cuffs on the gloves. This allows you to reach over the embers without having to expose the sensitive underside of your arms to the heat.

With the necessary gloves you can touch burning wood pieces.

*The roasting ther-
mometer does not
cost much, but
provides interesting
information*

Roasting thermometer

One of the most important instruments for beginning campfire cooks is a simple roasting thermometer. You don't have to show it to everyone, but you can secretly check the roast with it. Especially if you haven't gained much experience with cooking times yet, the interior temperature of the roast will tell you quite a bit about its state. Every piece of meat should reach at least 160°F (70°C) in the middle, before you can be sure it is not a health hazard. The thermometer is inserted into the thickest part of the meat, without touching a bone. After one minute you can read off the temperature.

> **Tip:**
>
> Especially with asado, you should measure the temperature in the legs. If the pig sits in the sun for seven hours, a lot of germs can develop, but at 160°F (70°C) all pathogens are killed off.

Skewers

Skewers are well suited to roasting a few small pieces of meat quickly. With the help of two baking stones a grill is quickly improvised. This way you can barbecue even at the hunting cabin, without tempting nonparticipants to barbecue during your absence, because of the grill stored there. Skewers that are flat and sharpened at the tip work very well.

Grill Grate

A proper grill grate has to be cast from cast iron. Only then will the meat reliably get the typical burn marks. Due to the large mass of the cast iron the items placed on it for grilling do not pull the heat out of the grate as fast. After a few seconds, the piece separates from the grill by itself. Also, cast iron does not warp and twist like grates welded from bars. On a stable grate, you should be able to place a coffee pot or a pan over the embers as well.

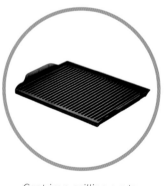

Cast iron grilling grate

Pot

To cook by the fire you don't necessarily need a Dutch oven, even if it is optimally suited for it. A simple cast iron pot or one made of tin will do; it just cannot have any plastic parts. Some stores carry pots made of Terracotta, which are handy for slow cooking at low temperatures. These pots are just placed near the fire

A tripod supporting a kettle

Copper kettles have the advantage over enamel that you can easily hammer out any dents.

You can easily determine the kettle size. You need one quart of pot content per person.

and turned occasionally. They heat up from the radiating heat of the fire or the stoked embers. An enamel roasting pan is ideal for preparing meat in an earth oven. For stews and beverages, copper kettles are well suited.

Tripod with Kettle

Even if, as mentioned before, setup with a tripod has disadvantages, the tripod cannot be matched as a holder for a heavy kettle. It stands much more stable and cannot tip to any side. If you want to purchase a tripod, you should use a specially made one and only put the bars together for exceptions.

A tripod should be at least 4 feet (1.20 meters) high for a 30 quart/liter kettle; 6 feet (1.90 meters) would be better, so that the kettle fits easily between the legs. The kettle is hooked onto the chain once. The distance to the fire is regulated by moving the legs of the tripod closer together or farther apart. The hook on the chain should be clamped so that it doesn't get accidentally unhooked when the kettle is attached and fall into the soup.

Even better than a chain with a hook is a so-called pothook or a kettle hook for the tripod. With this clever construction you can very easily adjust the filled kettle higher or lower, since the teeth of the kettle hook automatically lock into place. There is no fiddling involved as with the chain and hook.

A good tripod can easily be tested: Put it up and try to support yourself on it. The tripod must support your weight. Only such stable constructions are safe enough to be loaded with 60 pounds of boiling hot soup. Most tripods manufactured from pipes, the standard home improvement store variety, are not capable of this.

In order to be able to set up the tripod easily, two of the three rods should have an eyelet on top and at least one of the rods should have an open eyelet, as illustrated on the top right on p. 15. This way you have the options of setting up the rods as a tripod or with two rods pounded into the ground on the right and left of the fire and the third rod lying across the tops of them, above the fire. Since all tools for the campfire kitchen have a hook at the end, you can easily use this cross piece to hang up spoons, pans, and ladles.

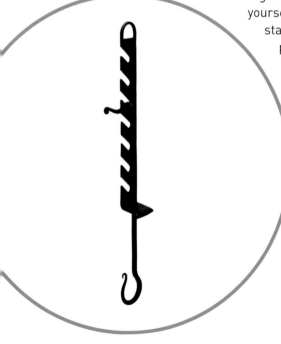

Kettle hook: better than any chain

Dough Scraper

A dough scraper is unbelievably handy for scraping out pots before cleaning them. You should always have this practical utensil handy.

Scooper (ladle)

Unfortunately, most households do not have a proper scooper, even though it is particularly important for outdoor use. When cooking for many people in a kettle by the open fire, this scooper should hold about one filling for a plate: 1-3/4 cups (400 ml). The handle of the scooper should be long enough so it cannot slide into the kettle. It should possess a hook at the end of the handle that you can use to hang the scooper on the fire structure. Setting something down in a clean setting is quite difficult in the outdoors.

Remove the food remnants from the pot with this simple dough scraper.

Fork

A long fork is a practical utensil for being far enough away from the heat of the fire when turning meat. You cannot purchase these forks. You have to have them made at the blacksmith's, since the "BBQ utensils" from the home improvement store are almost always unsuitable

Tongs

One of the first utensils you should acquire for cooking at the campfire is a proper set of metal grilling tongs. This tool is not just for grabbing the food, but also for rearranging the embers and pieces of wood. Look for good quality. I have seen BBQ tongs that were made of such thin metal that even small sausages slid out from their own weight. That kind is cheap, but useless.

Dutch Oven

A Dutch oven is a cast iron pot meant specifically for cooking by the open fire. Its special features are the flat bottom with the three legs and a lid with the raised edge. With the legs the Dutch oven sits above the embers, and the edge of the lid allows you to pile coal or embers on top of it in order to be able to cook the dish with top heat as well.

There are various manufacturers. The oldest one is the Lodge company from Tennessee in the USA. For over 100 years, they have been manufacturing the Original Dutch Oven from cast iron in the same traditional style. There are also Dutch ovens made of aluminum that, for various reasons, do not achieve results as good as the cast iron pots.

With BBQ tongs you can literally fetch chestnuts from the fire.

Operational principle of the Dutch oven: The heat penetrates uniformly from the top and the bottom.

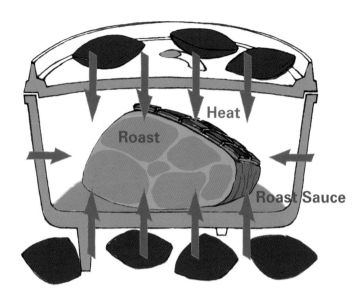

Dutch oven in the size 12 deep: The most popular model in Germany.

Lid Lifter

In order to be able to comfortably handle a Dutch oven, a lid lifter is necessary. Using the rod welded onto it crosswise at the bottom, the lid lifter wedges itself against the lid, and you can grab the lid securely and tightly even with a full load of glowing charcoal and deposit it or hang it up if necessary.

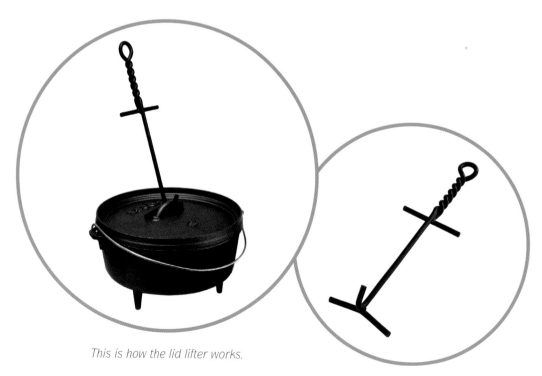

This is how the lid lifter works.

A lid lifter is required for cooking with a Dutch oven.

Conditioning Cast Iron

Cast iron pots and pans must be conditioned before their first use. However, the high quality Dutch ovens by Lodge are conditioned at the factory, so you can get going immediately with that brand. Other pots have to be conditioned first. First they must be washed in hot water and thoroughly dried. Then the entire surface area, while still hot from the warmth of the water, is rubbed with taste-neutral vegetable oil. Coconut oil is well suited for this. The warm material literally absorbs the oil.

When prepared like that, the cast iron is placed in the oven and remains there, at the highest temperature, for at least an hour. You should place plenty of aluminum foil underneath it to catch any dripping oil. Then turn the oven off and let the Dutch oven cool off inside. Conditioning works even better inside a kettle barbecue. You won't fill your kitchen with fumes either.

After this procedure you can rub in the oil one more time with a kitchen rag. The cast iron will have clearly darkened and, instead of a gray color, it will have taken on a dark brown, almost black coloration. During this treatment part of the oil evaporates and may spread fumes in your kitchen, so don't leave your kitchen during conditioning and ventilate it well.

Cast iron preconditioned at the factory can be recognized by its deep black color.

Conditioning works best in a kettle barbecue.

With use, cast iron takes on a black patina that also prevents food from sticking. You have to maintain it and take care of it. For cleaning, simply wash your Dutch oven with hot water. If food is sticking to it, fill the pot with water and place it over the embers again until the water boils. Most food can be removed with a brush; in extremely stubborn cases a sponge made of rust-free stainless steel mesh will help. You can also use a bit of salt for scrubbing, but then your oiled layer is ruined and your Dutch oven will have to be oiled again and reconditioned.

General Considerations for Cooking by the Campfire

For millennia, people only had the campfire for cooking. However, a lot of food can be prepared by a good fire with relatively little effort, if you observe a few tips. Never cook on the fire; but rather cook only over the embers, if possible. That way you won't burn your fingers when stirring the pot, and the pots won't be ruined with black soot. An open fire is too hot anyhow.

You should divide the cooking area: in one area you cook, in the other the campfire is burning and producing the required embers. The wood best suited for this is hardwood, such as beech or oak, conifer wood is less suited. The pieces of wood should be at most two fingers thick, since these will burn quickly and create hot embers, which you can then shovel onto the part of the fireplace which you want to use for cooking, using a small folding shovel.

Of course, you can also grill over the campfire. For this, let the fire burn down to embers, remove the last smoking wood pieces, and place the grill grate on two rocks above the embers. Generally, you only have enough time (actually embers) for one steak, then the fire will have expired, and you have to add new embers. You can barbecue longer using charcoal.

The typical cookware for the open fire was, and is, the Dutch oven. The term stems from America, where these pots, brought by German immigrants, have remained under the name "Dutch" or "Deutsch" (German). You place this cast iron pot with its three cast legs directly onto the embers, and place additional embers onto the lid to add top heat to the cooking process as well. You can prepare the famous baked beans in the Dutch oven, bake bread or cake, roast or braise meat, and, of course, cook stews. If you don't own a Dutch oven, you can cook by the open fire with any other pot—preferably a cast iron one.

Cooking by the fire means controlling the fire.

The Fire

If you wish to cook by the fire, you need to first start the fire. Once it is burning you still have enough time for preparing the food.

Let's move on to the fire. For millennia the fire in the middle of the house was not just the center of the house and the source of heat, but also the place where the food was prepared. Hence a warming fire differs significantly from a cooking fire. The heating fire is created to radiate as much heat as possible to the sides. It is built up high and burns with blazing flames. A cooking fire should be viewed as the complete opposite. There is no cooking fire per se, rather various types of fire that differ significantly based on the cooking method.

For cooking over the flames, a few pieces of wood the thickness of a thumb are quite sufficient. They are piled loosely on top of each other in the shape of a star and burn briefly and hot, for example, to warm up a pan on a tripod for browning.

To roast over the embers, you need a fire with hardwood pieces as thick as your arm. This fire, made of loosely piled wood pieces, only burns in order to use the embers it creates, whether it is for grilling over the embers, heating a Dutch oven, or cooking under the embers in aluminum foil. The embers are removed from under the wood pieces using a small shovel and placed in a slightly removed spot on the floor of the fireplace. This way you are away from the heat of the ember producing fire.

If something burns when cooking by the campfire, then it is always for one of two reasons: too much heat or not enough grease.

When a fire is older and has been burning for a few hours, ashes accumulate on the ground. These are another option for cooking, since they are able to insulate the heat from the fire and allow for uniform cooking of, for example, baked potatoes. So you should not continually remove the ashes from an open cooking area, but rather only remove the "excess" now and then.

You bury the items to be cooked in the ashes and cover them with more ashes before placing embers on top. This way you get, for example, baked potatoes without any burn marks and with a completely whole skin.

One kilogram of dried beech wood has a heat value of about 5 kW, but burns in 20 minutes when chopped into small pieces. Therefore, it is equivalent to a heat output of 15 kW/h; a standard cooktop manages at the most 2.3 kW/h.

Place two wood pieces as thick as your arm in parallel. On top of those pile pieces as thick as pencils and your thumb.

Underneath this construct place the tinder that you will ignite.

Once the pile starts burning, add further smaller wood pieces.

As soon as the lower construct collapses …

… place pieces as thick as your arm in the corner.

In as soon as an hour, you should be able to remove the first embers for cooking.

Tip:

In order to fry fish on the embers, the use of fish baskets is recommended. These are available at affordable prices and simplify turning without the fish falling apart.

ROASTING IN THE EMBERS

General Remarks

Roasting in the embers is actually the oldest form of cooking at the campfire. As a foundation, you need proper embers. You can only get these from dry hard wood. Conifer wood is not suitable. Loosely layer the wood pieces that are about as thick as your forearm and provide enough air in between the wood pieces that the fire burns without smoking. After a minimum of one hour, you can scrape together the embers.

When cooking on embers you should prepare a bed of embers about as thick as two fingers. The embers from a wood campfire are not as hot or as long lasting as the embers from charcoal. After about 20 minutes, they have cooled off and have to be replaced with new ones. Before setting the food into the embers, you should blow over them once to remove the small ash pieces. The wood you are burning for this type of cooking should be so clean that you would place the food directly onto the wood. Waste wood with varnish residue or railroad ties are taboo.

Ashes and charcoal are germ-free and not harmful. However, you should make sure that when eating there are no glowing pieces stuck to the cooked food!

A cooking fire is holy. Don't allow your guests to throw cigarette butts or used paper tissues into it. After all, you don't eat from the garbage pail either.

Bell Pepper in the Embers

A bell pepper prepared on the open fire is a delicacy. The bell pepper is simply placed on top of the embers or into the blazing fire until it is black all the way around and is creating bubbles. Then the black skin is simply rubbed off in a bucket of water until the pepper has returned to its original color. Afterward you cut the bell pepper into strips, spice them with salt and pepper, pour a bit of good olive oil on top, and then you just have to enjoy it.

> **INGREDIENTS PER PERSON**
>
> - 1/2 red bell pepper per person
> - Water for rinsing
> - Salt and pepper to taste
> - Olive oil

Place the bell pepper into the middle of the fire until its outer skin is completely black.

Put the pepper into a ready bucket of water.

In the water you can simply rub off the black skin.

After cutting slices simply spice with just pepper, salt and good olive oil.

Baking Potatoes

Some legends mention a traditional baking of potatoes. For this a large fire of beech wood is burned. The whole village participates. The side dishes are onion salad, coarse liver sausage, and pickled cream herrings. Generally, cold butter and salt are good enough.

The potatoes are placed directly onto the embers and have to "sweat." For this, smooth out the bed of embers with a shovel or rake and remove some embers from the middle to create an indentation. Place the potatoes into the indentation on top of the embers. After about 10–15 minutes, the potatoes start shriveling and can be covered up. Return the embers from the side back into the middle on top of the potatoes and let the potatoes cook for another half an hour. In between, you can fish out a potato and

For "sweating" the potatoes are placed on half of the layer of embers.

Then the potatoes are covered.

You can remove the potatoes after three quarters of an hour.

Traditionally the potatoes are rubbed clean with a towel and squished.

check whether it is soft yet. For this the potatoes are traditionally squeezed with the balls of your hands. They are eaten with their peel. During a large potato baking set-up, a solid cubic meter of wood is burnt up. The embers are then enough for two loads (about 20 pounds/10 kg each of potatoes.

Onions in the Embers

Barbecued meat is complemented fabulously by onions from the embers. You only need to place the onions with as much peel as possible on the embers and wait until they are fully cooked. Even though the outer layers burn, it doesn't matter. If you set the onions onto the embers with the roots pointing down and make sure that the upper "tip" does not burn, then you can peel the onions very easily when they are cooked. Simply pull apart the upper tip and the singed layers will loosen by themselves. You get a clean, soft onion with a wonderful aroma.

Onions directly on the embers.

Fennel in the Embers

Fennel is not to everyone's liking, but if you do like it, you should try preparing it on the embers. It is better to cut the fennel in half and roast it in a cast iron pan with the cut side facing down. Even though the consistency of fennel is relatively hard, because of its interesting taste it should not be missing from any plate of appetizers.

Fennel takes longer than other vegetables.

Surprise your guests with an appetizer plate. Cook onions, garlic, bell peppers, mushrooms, and eggplants on the embers.

Tomatoes

With tomatoes you can caramelize the cut surface in a cast iron pan.

Everyone knows grilled tomatoes. For the open fire, tomatoes aren't really suitable due to their relatively soft skin and the high water content. The tomatoes turn out better if you cut them in half and fry them on the cut side in an extremely hot pan. Simply place them onto the cut side and fry them until it is black. This caramelizes the fructose and lends a wonderful flavor.

Eggplants in the Embers

Eggplants are placed into the embers whole and roasted on all sides. For rotating them, either wear thick gloves or use long tongs. Even after just a few minutes, hot steam escapes from a tear in the skin, an unmistakable sign that the eggplant is done.

Take the eggplant out of the fire and cut it lengthwise with a sharp knife. Watch out for the escaping hot steam! Then brush the eggplant halves with cold-pressed olive oil and sprinkle them with pepper and salt. Figure half an eggplant per person as an appetizer.

The eggplant tears open and steams from the inside when it is done.

Cut open and seasoned with pepper, salt and olive oil it becomes an Italian appetizer.

Scallions in the Embers

Scallions are very rewarding vegetables. These can be prepared very easily directly on the embers since the long leaves form a natural handle. This way guests can help as well. Place the scallions directly onto the embers and turn the onions so that the outer layer chars. Then the onion is hot on the inside and has a delicious flavor. You only need to pull off the outer leaf before eating and then bite off the onion. You keep the green end in your hand.

Eggs in the Ashes

Eggs don't always have to be boiled. They are also a treat from the hot ashes of the campfire. The trick to this type of preparation is the long cooking time over many hours. The eggs take on a smoky flavor and an amber color. They are buried in the ashes of the campfire about two widths of a hand from the fire, so that they are cooked slowly by the heat radiating from the fire.

These eggs are also known as "Beitzah" and are a traditional meal for the Jewish Paschal festival.

Scallions provide their own handle in the form of their long green leaves. When the outer layer is black, the scallion is done.

The eggs are placed overnight into the cooling ashes of the campfire.

After twelve hours in the heat the eggs are brownish on the inside and taste nutty.

The portion-sized fish are placed directly onto the embers.

Trout in the Embers

Even though the skin no longer looks good, the meat tastes great.

Small, portion-sized fish, such as trout with a weight of about 1/2 pound (250–300 grams), are great for cooking directly on the embers. You are best off cleaning out the fish from the throat and avoiding the large stomach cut, but even with the stomach cut they can be grilled on the embers. Simply season the stomach cavity of the cleaned fish with salt, pepper, and lemon juice, and place the fish with its back to the fire onto the embers. The radiating heat from the fire will help cook the thicker back. After three minutes, the skin on the embers is black and dry. Then you turn the fish onto the other side, again with its back toward the fire. After another three to four minutes the fish is done. Even if the skin is no longer suitable for consumption, it is easy to remove. Larger fish are not suitable because they take longer to cook than their skin can take the heat. These should be cut in half and barbecued on a wood board (see p. 64).

The well-marbled steaks (at the most 1/4 inch thick) are placed directly onto the embers.

Steak in the Embers

Not only can steaks be prepared on the grill grate, but also directly on the embers. The meat takes on a mildly smoky flavor because of this. Only beef or game is suitable as the meat selection, since it is relatively dry. Pork and poultry release a lot of juices, and that extinguishes the embers. The meat is cut into thin (at the most 1/4-inch/0.5 cm thick) steaks and dried well. The meat must not be seasoned beforehand, since the spices will burn, and definitely not salted, since the meat juices will then escape and the charcoal will stick to the moist meat.

For the fire, which should be freshly burned down, hardwood or fruit woods are preferred. Before placing the meat on the embers, briefly blow into them so that the loose ashes fly away. Then the meat is grilled on both sides. When it is done, let it rest briefly on the plate and wipe off the attached charcoal pieces. Season with pepper and salt. Serve herb butter with it—and enjoy! Be careful not to put still-attached glowing charcoal into your mouth!

An old-fashioned cooking method for deer and red deer as well.

When the filling is cooking, the mushroom tops are done.

Mushrooms in the Embers

Larger mushrooms are particularly well suited for cooking in the embers. For this break the stems off the caps and drop a dollop of herb butter into each mushroom. When the mushrooms are bubbling inside, they are done. You should not roast too many mushrooms at once since they are done very quickly. It is best to remove the cooked mushrooms from the embers with tongs.

Chestnuts can be placed directly onto the embers.

Roasting Chestnuts

Edible chestnuts (sweet chestnuts) are dumped into a bucket with water. You remove the ones swimming on top since they are wormy. Then you cut a cross pattern into the shells with a sharp knife.

The chestnuts are then roasted in the embers or in a pan until they are soft. In a pan, that takes about 20 minutes; in the embers, only five to ten minutes. To eat them, peel the chestnuts and eat them with your hand. Caution: chestnuts not slit can explode with a bang in the embers and throw glowing pieces through the air!

Chestnuts are eaten with your hands.

Bruschetta

INGREDIENTS

- White bread
- Garlic
- Olive oil
- Salt

When your guests can do something themselves at the campfire, their joy and experience is multiplied. Bread roasts faster than meat or sausages. So here is a recipe that is not only easy but also tastes great.

For garlic bread, use fresh garlic that you simply cook on the embers for ten minutes. In order to have the skin withstand the fire until the garlic is cooked on the inside, you should soak the garlic bulb for half an hour in cold water beforehand.

Spread the soft garlic onto the fresh white bread slices and brush them with oil. Cold-pressed olive oil works well.

Then you poke the bread with a stick, a skewer, or a long fork and hold the slices over the embers.

Please be careful, however. In the beginning the slices do not change color but then they change very quickly, and if you don't pay attention, the bread will be black.

Don't cut your white bread into slices, but rather into pieces that you can then cut open lengthwise like a roll. This way you can poke the fork through the hard crust and not through the soft, doughy part as with a single slice.

The garlic is first soaked in water for two hours, then cooked on the embers until you can squeeze the interior out.

Then the bread is roasted with garlic.

COOKING UNDER
THE EMBERS

General Remarks

A minimum of one hand-width of fine sand is required in the fireplace!

Cooking under the embers is also a very old method. As early as the Stone Age, the hunters and gatherers set up fireplaces with fine sand at their campsites. And if no sand was available, then they carried it in. The sand and ashes of previous fires is needed to protect the food from the direct heat of the glowing charcoal. First you heat up the sand, then you shovel the embers to one side, the sand to the other side, then you put the food in, followed by placing the ash/sand mixture back over the food, at least as thick as two fingers, then the hot embers. Depending on the recipe, you can also have a brightly blazing fire on top of the buried food. That way you can maintain a defined heat: as hot as possible.

Potatoes and Onions Under the Embers

INGREDIENTS

• Potatoes and onions (the quantity per person depends on your hunger and the size of the potatoes)
• Salt
• Butter or herb butter

Potatoes and onions from the ashes, with their smoky flavor, bear no comparison to aluminum-wrapped potatoes baked in the oven. It is a simple meal where, nevertheless, much can go wrong. Who hasn't tried this as a child and come away with a product that was more reminiscent of coal than potatoes?

First light a big hardwood fire, so that plenty of embers are created. The fire should burn as long as possible, about two hours, so that the ground underneath the fire is heated up as well.

The embers are pushed aside with a shovel until the plain ground is visible. Push aside some of the ground with your shovel as well. Place the potatoes and onions in the resulting hollow. The onions should still have as much skin as possible; they are placed with the roots pointing down onto the hot ground.

The potatoes and onions are covered with the hot, dry dirt and the ashes. This is necessary so the potatoes do not turn into charcoal since they cannot sweat as when baking potatoes

Potatoes and onions are put into the ground, covered by a layer of ashes, then embers.

You can forget about potatoes under embers for half an hour without worries.

(see page 34). Pile about an inch of embers on top. Under no circumstance should you light a fire above the potatoes buried in the embers. That would be too hot.

> Count the potatoes beforehand, then you won't be searching as long when digging them out for that last potato that doesn't even exist.

After 45–60 minutes, carefully push the embers aside—the potatoes will be neither black nor charred—and test whether the potatoes are done. To do this, poke the potatoes with a fork or a knife. When digging out the potatoes you should proceed very carefully while wearing heat protective gloves so you don't damage the soft potatoes. If you try to work quickly using a folding shovel, you will soon have cut all of the potatoes in half and soiled them with sand.

Once the onions and potatoes are fully cooked, put the peeled onions on the plate. Rub the potatoes off with a towel and cut them in half. Add butter and salt or herb butter to the halves and spoon them out. This dish goes really well with pork tenderloin under the embers (see page 46). The advantage is that the potatoes do not need to cook very long and that you don't have to supervise the procedure; simply bury them and let them cook.

This procedure also works with other vegetables, such as red beets or even truffles.

Pork Tenderloin under the Embers

Pork tenderloin is particularly well suited for preparing it directly in the embers since the pieces are uniformly thick and large, so they cook evenly.

The tenderloin, with all sinews removed, is rolled in a mixture of dried herbs until the meat feels completely dry.

The fire is best pushed away from the hot ashes with a small shovel. Create a hollow about as deep as the thickness of two fingers, place the tenderloin in it and cover it with hot ashes. On top of that pile the embers, and on top of those the fire. By rekindling the fire, you get the highest temperature possible. After about 30 minutes, the meat is well roasted on the outside and still slightly pink on the inside. Now push the fire and the embers aside and lift the meat from the ashes. Only a very thin layer of ashes should actually be attached to it. You can easily remove those with a brush. You can rinse the meat in clear water, but you have to dry it off before cutting it. Don't salt and pepper the meat until after cutting it. Serve with potatoes and onions from the embers (see page 44).

First maintain a strong fire for about two hours, then ...

... place the herb coated tenderloin directly into the hot ash...

... and cover it one centimeter deep with white ashes.

Pile the embers from the fire on top, ...

... and maintain a strong fire on top of it for 30 minutes.

Then push the fire out of the way and take the tenderloin out of the ashes.

You cannot test the meat and then rebury it if it isn't done. Therefore, you are better off leaving it in the fire a bit longer rather than not long enough.

Rump Roast or Round Steak in the Ashes

INGREDIENTS

- 4-1/2 lbs rump roast or round steak, uncut
- 2 teaspoons crushed pepper
- 5 teaspoons Sugar
- 5 teaspoons Salt
- 1 teaspoon crushed chili flakes

Much to the delight of every gourmet, beef can also be roasted in the hot ashes. The taste is incomparable.

Mix the spices and roll the meat in a bowl with the spice mixture. The meat should be covered well all around and thus be dry on the outside. Store the meat in this coat of spices in the refrigerator at least overnight (two or three days is better). Dab the meat dry all around before roasting, push the fire aside and make a ditch in the ashes, then place the meat with the fat layer facing up. Cover the meat with at least two inches of ashes, pile plenty of embers on top, and maintain a very hot fire on top for about an hour.

The rump roast (or round steak) should keep the fat layer on top.

The meat, now rubbed with spices, should rest in the refrigerator overnight.

The rump roast is placed with the fat layer facing up into the hot ashes.

After about an hour the top side looks less enticing.

The bottom side is even darker, so the meat is washed in a bucket.

The aroma and the taste are simply indescribable!

Roasting Hazelnuts

Roasted hazelnuts
were our ancestors'
emergency food.

Hazelnuts have been calorie-rich nutrition for the winter since time immemorial. Our ancestors survived many food shortages with them. However, the fatty nuts are hard to digest raw, which can easily be fixed by roasting. For this, sand and a quickly lit fire are just right. Spread a layer of sand and, on top of that add the hazelnuts in their shells so they are touching but only in a single layer. Add another layer of sand on top, at least as deep as two fingers are wide. Light the fire using branches as thick as your thumb and let it burn down. Due to the thin wood the fire is very hot. Roast the nuts for about 20 minutes, then scrape the embers and the sand away.

There is a trick for cracking the nuts: Put the nut down on the rough area so the point is facing up. With a small rock carefully hit the tip. The shell will split into two halves without the kernel being mashed.

Line the fire pit with sand, place the nuts into it, and cover the nuts with two to three centimeters of sand. Build a fire using an armful of dry branches as thick as a thumb.

The nuts have improved considerably in taste and can be cracked easily.

The potatoes are covered with a layer of ash. On top of that layer add about 3/4 inch of embers.

ROASTING OVER THE EMBERS

General Remarks

Grilling food over the embers is usually our first connection with cooking over the campfire. If you use charcoal, then it is actually barbecuing. When using charcoal you have the advantage that the embers are hotter and last longer.

Heat at the campfire: Hold the back of your hand over the embers at the height where the meat is supposed to lay. Then count slowly. If you have to pull away your hand on three, then the embers are too hot; at five the fire is generally at the right temperature.

The embers from a hardwood fire release significantly more aroma than charcoal, so I prefer grilling over beech embers. These embers don't last long, however. You can really only grill one steak over the embers before you need new ones.

Roasting on a Spit

Cooking at the open fire is invariably associated with a spit rotating over the fire. Even if this image satisfies the adventurer in all of us, it cannot usually convince the gourmet. A rabbit or hare on the spit, for example, typically turns out dry.

If you still want to try roasting meat on a spit, you should place the supporting branch forks at the side of the fire since the meat is supposed to cook next to the flames in the radiating heat.

The spit should be as straight as possible and at least as thick as a thumb in order to be easier to handle. The meat is slid onto the spit and attached with wire and skewers. Make sure the meat is well attached since you cannot easily correct anything during the roasting.

The meat is not—as seen again and again in the movies—rotated continuously. Rather the spit is moved every few minutes in a quarter rotation. To do this, the spit should be stable in every position and not continue rotating on its own. With every rotation you brush the meat with melted butter or barbecue sauce, so it doesn't become too dry. A rabbit takes about half an hour, a hare about an hour.

A rabbit on the spit: It is possible, but there are tastier things.

Piglet on a spit: quickly prepared and delicious.

After two hours the food is ready.

Roasting larger animals, such as deer or suckling pigs, on such a natural spit is rather difficult. For this, professionally manufactured spits are better suited. You are better off choosing a different kind of preparation such as asado (page 144).

A piglet weighing about 11 pounds can still be handled without problems with a good hazel stick as thick as a thumb. A pig is cooked either over the embers or next to the fire. Here as well, a meat thermometer is helpful, because once the piece has been cut, it loses a lot of juice. Cook the meat first at low heat and then crisp the crust.

Poultry or winged game can be prepared in a tastier manner. For example, you can roast it on a rope (see page 62).

Meat Skewers

Original Russian Shashliks consist of pork neck that is marinated overnight in mineral water with a lot of carbonation. This makes the meat more tender.

To quickly grill small pieces of meat a skewer is particularly well suited. For a "grill" you only need rocks; two bricks placed lengthwise work particularly well. Shovel the embers under it and off you go. The embers from the campfire give the meat a special flavor that can only be achieved by the open fire.

The advantages of grilling skewers are that you don't need a grill and that you can immediately eat from the skewers with your hands. The skewers should be flat so the meat doesn't rotate on them. You should also sharpen the tips so threading them will be easier.

This recipe can be adjusted according to your mood and wishes or based on the availability of ingredients. For the meat you should pay attention to the quality, though. You need the bacon if the meat is lean, so the skewer does not turn out dry. The onions season the skewer.

You can use beef, veal, game, pork, or poultry for the skewer. As spices, large leaved varieties that can be threaded onto the skewer lend themselves to this, for example, laurel or sage leaves. Meat that is too dry should be marinated or at least brushed with oil.

INGREDIENTS PER PERSON

- 1/2 pound (200 g) meat (filet, neck)
- 1/4 pound (100 g) bacon
- 2 medium onions

Skewers can be prepared wonderfully at home and can be quickly grilled outside on two bricks.

Grilling Steaks

Cooking by the fire still means barbecuing for many people. A real steak can only be beef, preferably from a young bull that accumulated enough fat so that there are fat deposits between the meat fibers; this turns the meat soft and tender while roasting. For years now, I have preferred young bull entrecôte, known as "rib-eye steak" (because of the eye of fat). Cut at about an inch thick (3 cm), such a steak weighs nearly 1 lb and is enough for even a big eater. Also suitable is tenderloin or sirloin.

The selection of the meat is decisive for a successful steak that is juicy and tender inside. Your best choice is to buy from a butcher you trust because there are huge quality variations in meat. If you purchase the meat from an old milk cow labeled as beef roast, you get very lean meat that cannot turn tender when grilled. The fat between the muscle fibers is missing. However, if you purchase meat from a well fed young bull,you get steaks that are well marbled and will turn tender and juicy.

Good meat does not need to be marinated.

INGREDIENTS PER PERSON

- 1/2–1 lb (200–500g) meat (depending on appetite)
- pepper and salt
- herb butter

Marinade:

- 1/2 onion
- olive oil
- pepper

You have two options for barbecuing your steaks: either you simply place them on the grill or you marinate them. The easiest method for marinating meat is to season the meat on both sides with pepper and to set it into a glass bowl with onion rings. Then pour vegetable oil over the meat. Cold-pressed olive oil works particularly well for grilled steaks. Then place the meat in the refrigerator—it should not be excessively cold—and let the meat marinate for a day. Dab it dry before grilling and place it on a very hot grill. If you use a cast iron grate, the meat takes on the typical branding pattern. Barbecue for about five minutes on each side. When the meat gives a little upon pressure, then the steak is "medium.".

You recognize a good steak from its marbling.

On the cast iron barbecue grate …

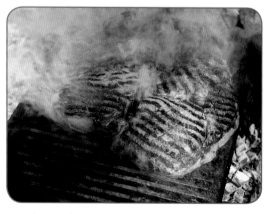

… the steak gets its branding pattern.

Upon cutting up to medium: a perfect steak!

Like the gauchos, barbecue your steak on a cast iron grate that you put on top of the embers that you remove from the fire. The embers do not have the same kind of heat you get from charcoal, but that is exactly what makes this a special art in barbecuing. Place the grate close to the embers so it can get extremely hot. Then place the meat on the grate. It will sizzle mightily. The cast iron grate has a big advantage over the cheap grates from the home improvement store: it stores large amounts of heat, so the meat cannot lower the temperature of the grate below 360° F (180° C). This is the temperature needed for roasting to create the great aromas, color, and taste.

When the meat is lying on the grill grate, it sticks to it and can't be loosened at first. Under no circumstance should you start loosening the meat with a knife or spatula, for when the steak is sufficiently grilled on this side, it will loosen by itself. So try it from time to time; if the meat can be lifted and doesn't stick any more, then turn it over. The meat will show you when it wants to be turned. If meat juices escape from the surface, the meat is

Purchase expensive, good sea salt and grind the pepper.

done and cooked medium inside. A perfectly grilled steak is only turned once and not constantly moved around, that is the trick.

The most important act for a good steak is the proper seasoning. Really, nothing but pepper and salt belongs on such high-quality meat. The pepper is freshly ground in the grinder and has a completely different aroma than the sneezing powder from the pepper shaker. The same applies to the salt as to the meat: Only the best is good enough. So do not use iodized salt or similar substances, but rather "fleur de sel," that quickly dissolves in the juice on the meat with its flat, scale-like crystals.

As a side dish you can serve potatoes, onions, and garlic bread prepared in the embers.

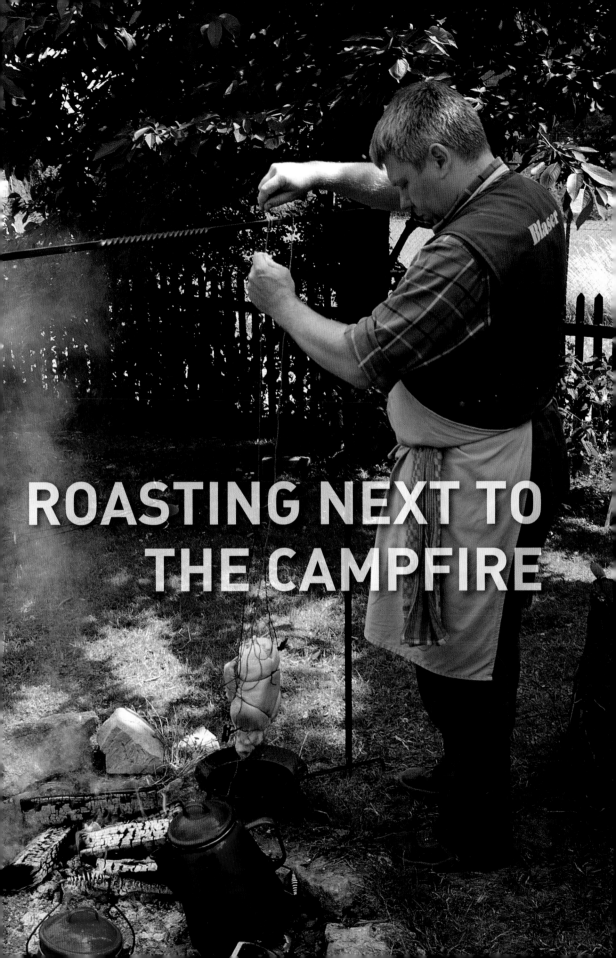

ROASTING NEXT TO THE CAMPFIRE

The string has to be at least three feet long, then the duck will rotate nicely (see the photo on page 61).

Duck on a Rope

INGREDIENTS FOR 4 PERSONS

- one duck (about 5 lb)
- 10 oz. (300g) ground pork
- 2 chopped onions
- plenty of majoram, mugwort, pepper, salt
- two metal skewers
- two wood skewers
- kitchen string (not plastic)

A duck roasted this way by the open fire is a particular specialty. It's convenient that with this type of preparation the duck—goose works too, but takes a long time—almost turns itself because of the long rope that it is attached to.

The duck is thoroughly cleaned inside and out. The ground meat is kneaded into a mass, together with the onions and spices, that is stuffed into the duck. Close the neck and back opening of the duck with the wooden skewers. With the two metal skewers poke through the duck from two sides and tie it up with the kitchen string so the duck's back end points upward. The bird is thus hung directly next to the fire by the string, which should be at least one meter long. Place a frying pan underneath the duck to catch the fat. The duck is now rotated several times around its own axis and let go. This way it rotates for a few minutes by itself because the rope will keep winding up and down.

The metal skewers are for hanging it up.

The duck is stuffed and the openings are closed up with the wooden skewers, then tied up with kitchen string.

Create a support system out of thin wire that you string through the metal skewers. Then you can conveniently hang the duck up with the back end facing up or down alternately.

With two wire loops the duck is attached quickly and can be adjusted.

The cooking time is at least three hours. Most campfire cooks get restless during their first attempt, because nothing seems to be happening. What is really happening in this type of preparation? The fire should be very hot. To check this, the back of your hand to the fire at the height of the duck and start counting slowly. If you have to remove your hand when you reach three, the fire is just right.

The duck is usually attached at a refrigerator temperature of about 45° F (7° C). The skin and the protein change visibly, but not until 140° F (60° C), so the fire has to achieve a temperature increase of 95° F (53° C) for you to see anything. Getting up to a core temperature of 175° F (80° C) is then only another 35° F (20° C) difference, so more than half of the increase already achieved.

This method also works for turkeys, geese, as well as legs of deer and lamb.

The duck on the rope has two disadvantages and two advantages: it does not turn properly brown or properly crisp, but the taste is delicious and the meat is indescribably tender.

In the collected fat you can fry potatoes, onions, and other vegetables. However, you should shield the frying pan from the fire with a brick until it is time for frying, so it doesn't get so hot from the radiating heat that the duck fat burns.

Take some nails about 4 inches long and hammer them in with a few relaxed hits. They don't have much to hold. The trick is to use lots of nails.

The nailed-on salmon is rubbed with a spice mixture.

Salmon on a Board

Simply nail the salmon filet with the tail pointing up and the skin against the board. Season with plenty of crushed juniper berries, pepper and salt, and place with the board by the fire. After 20 minutes, carefully check whether the meat can already be easily removed with a fork. Salmon tastes best fresh off the board.

INGREDIENTS FOR 4 PERSONS

- salmon filet (around 2 lb [1 kg])
- mixture of 2 tablespoons salt, pepper, and juniper berries
- an untreated board (soaked in water for at least two hours)
- some nails, not galvanized

COOKING BY
THE CAMPFIRE

Beverages

For many, preparing a multi-course menu is not the rule; rather, their cooking is limited to a hot beverage requiring little effort. But it revives the spirits at the right time and especially in winter provides heat from the inside.

Campfire Coffee

A good breakfast should include good coffee like the cowboys drink it. This coffee does not need to be filtered since the coffee grounds settle on the bottom when you pour half a cup of cold water into the boiling hot coffee.

A question asked over and over again is the one about the proper kind of coffee. Simply use vacuum-packed coffee for common coffee machines.

Fill the pot with water (at most, up to the bottom of the spout) and add the measured coffee grounds. Bring to a boil at the campfire. Then remove from the fire and add half a cup of cold water, so that the coffee grounds will settle. Pour into cups and enjoy.

You place the pot with the handle facing away from the fire (which keeps the handle cool) at the edge of the campfire. It can sit in the embers.

Watch out when pouring! If the pot is only half full and the front is very hot, the coffee will spurt far out of the pot! If the coffee starts tasting bitter with time, top it off with some cold water to replace the evaporated liquid.

INGREDIENTS PER CUP

- 1 cup water
- 2 teaspoons ground coffee

For the large pot containing about gallon, use about one heaping coffee cup of coffee powder.

Wine Punch

Winter is the season for wine punch and copper kettles are ideal for its preparation.

Heat the red wine and the orange juice in a 2 to 3 quart copper kettle (do not let it boil). Then remove it from the fire and attach the sieve for the cone of sugar. Set the cone of sugar into the sieve, pour the rum over it slowly so it can properly absorb it and the rum doesn't instantly drip into the wine. Let it burn off. You have to refill several times during the burning-off process. Very important: Never pour the rum from the bottle directly onto the cone of sugar, the bottle could explode in your hand. Always use a ladle to pour the rum over the sugar. Have a 10-liter bucket of cold water ready and dip the ladle into it every time before adding rum, to cool it off and to extinguish the flames. And even more important: Have a fire extinguisher and a fire blanket ready since: "It's better to have and not need it than to need it and not have it!" Very important accessories are the heat protection gloves since the sugar sieve will get hot and has to be removed before you can get to the punch.

For a larger kettle multiply the amounts.

INGREDIENTS FOR A 10-LITER POT

- 5 qts (5 l) red wine
- 1 qt (1 l) orange juice with pulp
- 1 cone of sugar (about 1/2 pound)
- 1 pt (0.5 l) rum (100 proof)

Caution, the sieve is extremely hot after the cone of sugar burns off. You cannot loosen the screw without gloves.

Quick Breakfast for the Hiker with Little Luggage

The Billy can gets its name from the tea variety "Billy-Tea" that Australian migrant workers made in it.

How often do you feel like having something warm in your stomach while hiking? With a Billy can and a pan you can quickly prepare something for yourself. The trick here is the fire: it is built with branches no thicker than your thumb. First you build a holder for the Billy can. Here, also, freshly cut branches as thick as your thumb work well. In addition to the cross branch that is about three feet long, you also need a branch with a fork cut to a short length and a longer branch with a fork since this one is pushed into the ground. Carve a notch into the cross branch so the handle of the Billy can doesn't slide off. Then you stick the longer branch fork into the ground next to the planned fire, place the cross branch into it and secure it with the second branch fork. Then use the filled pot to test whether your construction holds up. Only then do you light the fire.

Here we chose a wood splinter as underlayment for a few pine shavings. Using a fire steel, this is quickly lit. On top of this place the shavings created when the sticks were made, then the four prepared sticks that now look as if they had curls. After less than one minute the flames should be flickering as high as the width of a hand above the wood. With a few pencil-thick wood pieces you will quickly have an extremely hot fire going, which will bring the water in the Billy can to a boil within a few minutes. After that add a few pieces of wood or splinters the thickness of your thumb. Once the water is boiling you can prepare tea, coffee, a broth, or even a sausage with it. Then it's time for the frying pan (see the illustrations on p. 70). Two pieces of wood as thick as your arm are ideal as pan topping and are always available in a forest. This wood should be dry because it doesn't smoke as much as moist wood. It is not necessary to use fresh wood since everything happens so fast that even pieces as thick as your arm do not burn up before the food is done.

Preparation

Place the bacon, without grease, into the dry and cold pan and let it fry slowly. Once it has shrunk and the underside is brown, turn the bacon slices over. The bacon must be removed from the pan because it doesn't become crispy until it cools off. The sunny-side-up eggs are fried in the bacon grease along with, if so desired, some bread as well. You can also bake the sourdough pancakes (see the next recipe) in the pan since they absorb the grease nicely.

INGREDIENTS

• bacon and eggs as needed

The holder for the Billy can.

First test the durability of the cooking stand without a fire.

Some of the pine shavings onto an underlayment.

The sticks that look as if they have curls are prepared.

The first shavings burn.

The curly sticks are the next layer.

The fuel consists of branches with a maximum thickness of a thumb.

Add the fuel to the fire.

After less than a minute the pot is surrounded with flames. .

When the fuel has burned down, the water in the Billy can is boiling.

Two logs as thick as your arm are the support for the pan with bacon.

The bacon fries.

Two fried eggs round off the meal.

Everything is eaten out of the pan.

The pancakes fry in the bacon grease.

The legendary American breakfast consists of bacon and eggs served with sourdough pancakes with maple syrup. All you need for this is a large grilling plate or a large pan. We use a Lodge cast iron pan and a grill grate. The pancakes taste hearty and very nutritious due to the sourdough. The maple syrup is not very sweet and goes well with it.

Sourdough Pancakes

In a bowl, mix together the ingredients with a fork and put them aside in a warm location for an hour until the dough forms bubbles. For baking, the dough is spooned into the hot frying pan with grease, one spoonful at a time. Let the pancakes brown briefly on one side, then flip them and brown them on the other side too. The pancakes that are about as thick as a finger should be light and have a slight sourdough taste.

If the taste is too sour for you, you can reduce the taste with a teaspoon of baking soda.

INGREDIENTS FOR 12 PANCAKES

- 2 cups sourdough
- 1 cup wheat flour
- 1 cup water or milk
- 1 lightly beaten egg
- 2 teaspoons oil
- 2 teaspoons sugar
- 1 pinch salt
- maple syrup

Tip

Sourdough is available in well-stocked supermarkets sealed in plastic bags. Add the content of one of these bags to the same amount of rye flour in a bowl the day before and add enough water to make the dough as fluid as waffle batter. The next day, the sourdough will be nice and frothy at room temperature.

Beans in a Bottle

**INGREDIENTS
FOR ONE**

- 24 oz. (0.7 l) bottle
- 2 cups dried white beans
- 1 teaspoon salt
- 1–3 garlic cloves
- water
- 1/2 cup cold-pressed olive oil

For this dish you need a bottle with as large a neck as possible and a campfire that will burn for a few hours since the cooking time can easily be six to eight hours. You are compensated for this with a taste adventure without a match—and that with a dish that takes no effort.

The bottle is filled halfway with white beans that have not been soaked. Then you add salt, garlic and olive oil, fill the bottle to 3/4 with water, and place it right next to the fire.

The bottle is sealed with a folded kitchen towel. If the water evaporates during preparation, you refill it carefully so the bottle does not crack.

Once the potatoes are brown on one side, you add the bacon.

Then cook everything until the bacon is crisp too.

Fried Potatoes

Good fried potatoes require fat! Take as large a pan as possible and heat a lot of lard or clarified butter in it. Then add the potato slices. It's best to add these one at a time, so that they lay flat in the pan and have contact with the iron. Don't add anything else at this point or everything will burn. When the potatoes are crunchy on one side, carefully turn each one over individually and fry them until crisp on the other side as well. Once the potatoes are half done, add the bacon and onion cubes. It is important now to move the pan around or to stir the potatoes if the pan is too heavy.

As soon as the onions become glazed, season with pepper and salt, a bit of ground caraway, and a lot of marjoram.

INGREDIENTS PER PERSON

- lard for frying
- 1/2 cup bacon cubes
- 1/2 cup onion cubes
- 2 large boiled potatoes, sliced
- marjoram, ground caraway, pepper, and salt

Pork Tenderloin in Pepper Sauce

An excellent dish for company that can be prepared in a large pan and multiplied easily. You need pork tenderloin, onions, green peppercorns from a jar (or can), and sauce bernaise—since this is a dish for large groups, you should fall back on premade sauce.

Melt the clarified butter in a large pan, brown the tenderloin that has been cut into medallions, then sauté the diced onions and the mushrooms, as well as the peppercorns, until the liquid has evaporated. Finally, deglaze it with the sauce; if necessary replenish the evaporated liquid with water, so the sauce has the right consistency.

> Green pepper from a can or jar is preserved in a vinegar salt brine. Before use, pour the content of the can into a sieve and rinse the liquid off. The drained peppercorns are then added to the pan for sautéing and brought to a boil. This removes the sour taste.

INGREDIENTS PER PERSON

- 10 oz. (300g) pork tenderloin
- one small onion
- 1/2 teaspoon green peppercorns (without brine)
- 1/2 cup (100 ml) Sauce Bernaise
- clarified butter for frying
- fresh mushrooms, if available

As side dishes, fresh white bread or potato wedges or Rösti (Swiss hash browns) from the oven taste good.

The large pan by Lodge, with its 17" diameter, can easily hold 6-1/2 pounds of meat, an amount sufficient for ten people.

This dish can easily be eaten out of a bowl if you don't have enough places to sit at a table in the forest. Then you simply cut the meat smaller, into bite-sized chunks, and hand out spoons. For the preparation you merely need a pan and the chopped ingredients in sealed containers. First brown the meat in the pan by portions, remove it and store in a bowl. Then brown the onions and the mushrooms, depending on the capacity and heat performance of the pan, also by portions. Whatever you remove, you can add to the bowl with the meat. Then add the green peppercorns and let them boil so the liquid evaporates. Return the remaining ingredients to the pan and pour in the sauce. Since sauce bernaise is quite dense, thin it with water or cream if necessary. If the sauce turns out to be too thin later on, simply let some liquid evaporate.

Hunter's Stew

INGREDIENTS FOR 4–6 PERSONS

- 1 lb (500g) ground meat
- oil for frying
- 1 onion
- 1 bell pepper
- 1/2 lb fresh mushrooms
- pepper and salt
- 1 lb (500g) potatoes
- 1/2 lb (250g) cheese for gratinating

The Hunter's Stew is a typical stew that turns out extraordinarily tasty in either a pot or a pan. If you use a frying pan, then you should use one with a lid. It works without a lid too, but the cheese won't melt as nicely.

First brown the ground meat well in a bit of oil. Add the diced onion and the bell pepper, as well as the sliced mushrooms, and brown them. Then season with pepper and salt and remove from the pot.

Cover the bottom of the pot with the peeled and sliced potatoes and add the ground meat-vegetable mass back in. Pour in a bit of water and cook the potatoes until soft with a bit of heat from below until the water evaporates.

At last, sprinkle the cheese over the whole thing, put the lid on top and gratinate it with a lot of heat from above until the cheese melts and is brown.

Instead of the potatoes you can also use ready-made mashed potatoes.

Mushroom Pan

INGREDIENTS PER PERSON

- 7–10 oz (200–300g) fresh mushrooms, preferably chanterelle
- 1 small onion
- 2 oz (50g) smoked bacon, diced
- 4 tbsp (50g) clarified butter for frying
- pepper and salt

Mushrooms by the open fire are a very special delicacy, especially if you collected the mushrooms yourself. For chanterelle, it is important that they are properly browned in fat since they don't develop their typical taste until they reach over 350° F (180° C).

Heat the clarified butter and bacon in the pan then remove the bacon. Add the chopped onion and sauté until translucent. Now add the fresh, cleaned mushrooms as well as the pepper and salt.

Stew the mushrooms in the fat while stirring continuously until they stop simmering. You can make some room in the pan and fry some eggs or a round steak. By adding a cup of cream you end up with creamed mushrooms. If you then add a litter of beef broth, you have cream of mushroom soup.

A Quick Meal

If you are in a hurry, then a grill works well. The charcoal can warm up on its own, while you prepare the meat.

Season 1/2–2/3 pound (250–300g) of pork neck per person, using rotisserie spices and applying heavily on both sides. Place the spices on a plate and roll the moist meat in the spice mixture, so it is "coated" well on both sides.

Put the baked beans in a pan and heat them slowly on the grill. Barbecue the meat on both sides. Toasted bread goes well with it, and so does a cool beer.

INGREDIENTS PER PERSON

- 1/2–2/3 lb (250–300g) pork neck
- rotisserie spices
- 1 small can baked beans
- bread or rolls

Egg Sunny-side Up

A simple method for frying a single egg for a meal is to break it over a hot stone on which a piece of bread with a hole in it is lying. The egg cannot run and cooks on the stone. You can then remove the breakfast from the stone with a spatula: toast and fried egg at the same time. Of course, this method also works in a pan.

FOR CHILDREN

You can prepare popcorn in a Dutch oven.

Popcorn

Cover the bottom of the Dutch oven with oil and heat from below. Sprinkle in the popcorn, so that the bottom is, at the most, half covered and every kernel has contact with the bottom. Put the lid on top and wait until the popping ends. You may want to stir it occasionally with a wooden spoon since popcorn burns easily. Remove the popcorn from the pot and sprinkle it with salt or sugar in a bowl.

However, there are also special "popcorn machines" for campfires

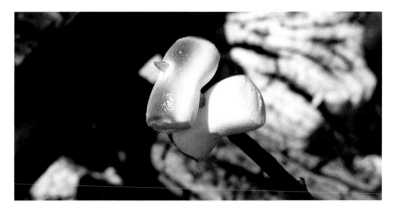

Childhood experiences you never forget: Adventures in the outdoors.

Marshmallows

An absolute high point for children at the campfire is to be able to hold something into the flames and to roast it. This is exactly what marshmallows are great for. Roasting them is fast and always works. Marshmallows do not make fat stains and are nice and sweet. They are simply speared and held carefully by the embers. Once they turn brown, they have to be eaten quickly, otherwise they drip.

Children love simple things: sausages, bacon and marshmallows

Frying Bacon

Holding something by the fire with a stick or a fork fascinates young and old. Since not everyone likes the sweet marshmallows, suitable alternatives are bacon, hot dogs, or sausages. Bacon is fried in the heat radiating from the fire and the escaping grease is spread on bread.

Bread on a Stick

At every event with an open fire, bread on a stick seems to be present. Its popularity, however, seems to be in strong contrast to the consistently modest result. Children generally do not have the patience to bake the dough properly. And even then bread on a stick still tastes like pizza dough without toppings

To eliminate the majority of mistakes, you should either use the pizza dough from page 119 or fall back on chilled, ready-made dough that you roll out to a thickness of just 1/8 inch (3mm), and roll around the stick with a slice of bacon in the shape of a spiral. For baking you hold the stick close to the embers, under no circumstances—as is often seen—into the flames.

COOKING IN A DUTCH OVEN

Bird with Vegetables

The Dutch oven is practically made for poultry. While it doesn't turn crispy, it does turn out wonderfully juicy. Depending on the size of the pot and your appetite use one or several roasting chickens, pheasants, pigeons or whatever you choose.

Salt and pepper the bird on the inside and outside; sprinkle with poultry spices if desired. Pour olive oil into the Dutch oven so that the bottom is covered. Add a bit of water if the vegetables are very dry. Place the poultry into the pot on its back and add the vegetables. Salt and pepper everything (if you love it hot, add a chili pepper). If you so desire, add corn on the cob or corn kernels out of the can, and also any vegetable you have handy. With this dish, the exact amounts are not that important.

The Dutch oven is left to its own devices in the embers with plenty of top heat for one to one-and-a-half hours. Nothing bad happens if you extend the time a bit. It is just important that enough liquid remains in the pot, so nothing burns. Even though the bird does not become crispy, it does turn fabulously tender and juicy.

INGREDIENTS FOR ABOUT 4 PERSONS

- 2-1/2 lb (1,200g) poultry (chicken, pheasant, pigeon)
- 2 quartered onions
- 1 bell pepper in strips
- 1 carrot
- 2 potatoes in small pieces
- corn
- salt and pepper
- olive oil

Place the chicken in the pot and add the vegetables..

After about an hour the chicken is done.

Chili con Carne

A typical campfire dish is chili. You can create large quantities of it relatively easily. The dish benefits from long cooking times. To be flexible in the number of people and to accommodate cooking outdoors, you will find the quantity ratios here along with the quantity specifications. For good chili it is important to use plenty of meat. Chili is served with onion rings, shredded cheese, and canned hot pepper.

Deeply brown the crumbled ground (or minced) meat in oil in a Dutch oven, then add the onion cubes and let them turn translucent. Don't season until then, but then go ahead and season heavily. Add the strained tomatoes and the drained beans and let everything cook for about 30 minutes with low top and bottom heat. Add some water if the mass is too dry. Right before the end of the cooking time, season to taste again and add the corn, but just let it get hot so it stays nice and crunchy.

If you use Tabasco for seasoning, you need to bring the chili to a boil again, so the vinegar taste dissipates.

Sprinkle the meat with some sugar while browning then it will take on a nice brown color more quickly.

INGREDIENTS FOR ABOUT 4 PERSONS

- 1/2 lb (200g) ground meat (2 parts)
- 1/2 lb (200g) chopped onion (2 parts)
- 1/2 lb (200g) red beans (2 parts)
- 1/4 lb (100g) corn out of the can (1 part)
- 1 cup pureed tomatoes (1 part)
- pepper and salt
- oil
- chili
- caraway
- paprika powder or spice mixture

Chili is traditionally served with shredded cheese and onion rings.

Potatoes as a Side Dish

INGREDIENTS PER PERSON

- 1–2 large potatoes
- 1/2–1 onion
- 1/4 lb (100g) bacon
- grated cheese for gratinating
- pepper and salt
- 1 cup cream

Potatoes out of the Dutch oven are a filling and quickly cooked side dish. If you don't want the potatoes to be quite as heavy, replace the cream with milk.

In a 14" Dutch oven you can cook potatoes for 15 people. If you add more bacon, you have a tasty main meal.

Dice the bacon and the onions and cut the peeled potatoes into slices. First place a layer of potatoes into the Dutch oven, put onions and bacon bits on top, and season it well with salt and pepper. Depending on your taste you can add other spices, such as hot paprika powder and others.

Then you place the next layer of potatoes, followed by bacon and onions, with the last layer being a layer of potatoes. At the end, pour the cream on top so that the Dutch oven is about half full.

The potatoes should first cook in the steam. Place the lid on the Dutch oven and cover it with embers. The potatoes need about 20 minutes until they are done.

Next sprinkle the cheese on it and wait until it has melted and turns light brown. Serve the Dutch oven potatoes as hot as possible. Whether as a side dish or a main meal—they always taste good.

Layer the ingredients in the Dutch oven.

At the end let the cheese melt using top heat.

Stew

INGREDIENTS FOR 4 PERSONS

- 2 lbs (1kg) diced beef
- 1/2 lb (250g) bacon
- 1 lb (500g) carrots
- 2 lbs (1kg) potatoes
- 2 bell peppers
- 1 cup soy sauce
- 5 medium celery sticks
- 2 onions
- 1/2 cup Worcestershire sauce
- Tabasco
- pepper and salt
- oil for frying

This stew is particularly well suited when you have more time for cooking or if you wish to cook more portions to reheat later.

First heat the oil in a Dutch oven and start frying the meat and the diced bacon in it. Peel the vegetables and cut them into pieces. Then add the onions and fry them. Next add the rest of the ingredients and cook until the vegetables are tender. Season to taste and serve. This dish can certainly be prepared in the morning and cooled down in the campfire. In the evening you merely have to heat up the food. It tastes even better then.

Prepare the vegetables (cut into pieces).

First fry the meat and the bacon.

Then add the other ingredients.

Let the dish simmer for at least two hours.

Before serving, you should season it once again.

Cowboy Beans

In one tablespoon of butter or olive oil, brown the diced bacon in the Dutch oven. Add the diced onions and sauté them in the bacon until they are translucent.

Fill the pot with soaked beans. You are best off seasoning with Maggi Texicana, a sauce with lots of chili powder. Add pepper, salt, sugar, mustard, sambal oelek, and tomato paste. In such dishes, the sweet note is often forgotten, leaving them spicy but somehow tasting bland. So a bit of sugar or sweet tomato paste must be added. You pile embers on the lid to get top heat. Let the whole thing simmer for three to four hours, until the beans are done. By the way: this dish tastes best reheated.

INGREDIENTS FOR 6–8 PERSONS (AS A SIDE DISH)

- 3 cups beans, soaked the day before (one cup each kidney, pinto and white beans)
- 2 cups diced bacon
- 3 cups diced onions
- 1 cup chili sauce
- 1 can tomato paste
- 2 teaspoon mustard
- 1 tablespoon sugar
- pepper and salt
- sambal oelek
- butter or olive oil

Food for hungry cowboys.

Goulash

INGREDIENTS FOR ABOUT 6 PERSONS

- 2 lbs (1kg) stew meat
- 1/2 lb (250g) diced smoked bacon
- 1 can (450 ml) peeled tomatoes
- 5 onions, coarsely diced
- 1 each red, green, and yellow bell peppers
- 1 teaspoon each thyme, caraway, majoram, ground pepper
- 2 teaspoons fine sweet paprika powder
- 1 teaspoon salt
- 1 teaspoon Fondor (universal seasoning)
- 1 can chanterelle mushrooms

Thoroughly brown the meat and the diced bacon on all sides in the lid of the Dutch oven or in a pan, one serving at a time. Transfer it into the Dutch oven or into a kettle and add the spices. Fry the onions along with it until they are translucent. Then add the sliced bell peppers and let them sauté.

Add the peeled tomatoes (with liquid) and an additional quart of water (or, even better, broth), put the lid on, and place six to ten glowing pieces of coal on top. Let the goulash simmer for two hours. With this dish it doesn't matter if the pot gets cold in between or if the coal has ceased glowing. You can also leave the pot in the cooling campfire while you, for example, go hunting.

When the goulash is done, brown the chanterelle mushrooms on the upside down lid, then mix them into the goulash. Season the whole thing with paprika powder, pepper, and salt.

For the chanterelle to develop their aroma or to set them free, they must be heated in hot grease to over 360° F (180° C).

Tip:

Goulash tastes good with fresh bread or noodles, and also a red country wine or beer.

Spicy Bean Soup

Heat olive oil in the Dutch oven and brown the ground meat in it. Remove the browned ground meat from the Dutch oven and brown the onions in fresh olive oil. Put the browned meat back into the pot. Cut the tomatoes (still in the can) several times with a long knife and put them in the Dutch oven; dissolve the soup cubes in the saved juice and add it to the Dutch oven as well. Then add the bell pepper strips (with juice) and the other bean varieties (with juice). Season with the spices and let it cook for at least half an hour.

INGREDIENTS FOR ABOUT 15 PERSONS

- 2 lbs (1kg) ground meat (or minced)
- olive oil for frying
- 2 lbs (1kg) onions, coarsely diced
- About 1/2 lb (500g) white beans from the can
- About 1/2 lb (500g) red kidney beans from the can
- 1/2 lb (500g) chili beans from the can
- 2 large cans (2 lbs) peeled tomatoes
- 1 large jar sour, pickled red bell pepper strips
- 2 teaspoons paprika powder, premium sweet
- 2 teaspoon salt
- 2 teaspoons ground pepper
- chili powder to taste
- soup cubes for 2 qts liquid

With this stew serve homemade bread and a cool beer.

Pound Stew

This dish exists in different versions. It has a great advantage over other goulash dishes: the meat is not browned first. Rather, all ingredients are layered into a pot and then cooked.

This dish can be prepared in a Dutch oven, in a kettle over the fire, or in a roaster that you place on two bricks over the fire. It is important to cook slowly with low heat.

Cut the meat and bell peppers into small pieces, finely chop the onions and garlic, and put them in the pot. Form cherry-sized balls out of the ground meat and put them in the pot as well. Then add the tomatoes, chili sauce, cream, and the spices, and carefully mix everything. First, heat the Dutch oven with embers under the pot and then continue cooking the dish with a lot of top heat (then it won't burn).

INGREDIENTS FOR 10 PERSONS

- 1 lb smoked pork neck
- 1 lb beef goulash
- 1 lb pork cutlet meat
- 3 bell peppers
- 1 lb onions
- 1 lb ground meat
- 1 large can tomatoes (with juice)
- 1 bottle chili sauce
- 3 cups cream
- 2 teaspoons paprika
garlic
- pepper and salt

Tip:

If you are cooking this dish in a kettle, start with low heat and maintain it, since the dish is not supposed to be stirred. Pound stew takes about three hours before the meat is tender.

One pound is equivalent to half a kilogram.

Baked Camembert

An appetizer from the Dutch oven that has you longing for a second helping.

Spread the puff pastry such that it can easily be folded over the camembert. Line the Dutch oven with several layers of aluminum foil. Set the camembert in the middle of the puff pastry, surround it with currants, and fold the puff pastry together over the camembert. At the top there should be an opening so the steam can escape and the puff pastry will turn crispy. Brush the puff pastry with egg yolk and bake for a quarter of an hour in the Dutch oven with a lot of top heat, until the puff pastry is golden and the cheese runny.

INGREDIENTS FOR 2 PERSONS

- 1 lb camembert
- puff pastry (frozen product)
- 2 tablespoons currants from the jar
- 1 egg yolk for brushing

Spare Ribs

INGREDIENTS PER PERSONS

- 1 to 1-1/2 lb (500–800g) spare ribs with bones
- grease for frying
- barbecue sauce from the bottle
- honey for coating

Spare ribs are available in supermarkets, but if there isn't enough meat on them, you can also take real rib meat that is cut into pieces along the ribs. It is important to remove the solid silver skin from the inside, because it never becomes tender, even when cooked for a long time.

Brown the ribs in the Dutch oven in hot grease, cover with barbecue sauce, and let it simmer for an hour. Then, when the sauce has become nice and thick, coat the ribs with honey, then brown another ten minutes with plenty of top heat.

If you own a second Dutch oven, you can bake fresh bread to go with it.

Chicken Breast in Cream Sauce

In the Dutch oven's upside down lid, heated in the embers, brown the chicken breasts without skin one after the other (you can also use pork or turkey cutlets). At the same time, brown the onions and the cleaned and sliced mushrooms in the Dutch oven. Once the chicken breasts are browned, they are placed in the Dutch oven and seasoned with salt and pepper.

In a large bowl, stir together the cream and the crème fraîche with the spices. Pour this over the chicken breasts, cover with the lid, and put the Dutch oven on the embers. Heat with just a few embers (six to eight pieces of glowing coal) from the bottom for the first hour, until the meat is tender. Then brown the breasts with plenty of top heat for half an hour to an hour. The sauce should be getting thick.

INGREDIENTS FOR 5–6 PERSONS

- 10–12 chicken breast filets
- 1/2 lb (500g) onions in slices
- 1/2 lb (500g) fresh mushrooms
- pepper and salt
- 2 cups cream
- 2 cups crème fraîche
- 1 teaspoon curry
- 1 teaspoon paprika powder
- clarified butter for frying

Tip:

An even easier variation: Brown the breasts in the Dutch oven, then simply stir cream and crème fraîche into canned onion soup and cream of mushroom soup and add to the meat. As side dishes, rice or bread work well; as beverages, a light, white summer wine or rosé go well, as does, of course, beer.

If you want to, you can also cover the entire thing with cheese, which makes the meal even more sumptuous.

Rotisserie Roast

INGREDIENTS PER
PERSONS

• 2/3–1 lb (300–400g) pork
neck roast without bones
• sunflower or olive oil
• rotisserie spices
(1 tablespoon per pound)
• onions (1 lb per lb meat)

A very thick roast should
be scored lengthwise, so
the spices can penetrate
into the middle.

This is a very easy recipe which, nevertheless, delivers convincing results. Since rye rolls go really well with it, it makes sense to bake them right along with it (see page 112). The two Dutch ovens are then placed on top of each other; the embers on the lid of the bottom one are then simultaneously the bottom heat for the upper Dutch oven.

Mix the oil with the rotisserie spices until you have a thin paste. Mix it with the onions, coarse-cut into slices, until the individual onion slices are well moistened. Now put a layer of the onion-oil-spice mixture into a glass bowl (plastic can discolor), place the roast on top, and distribute the remaining onion-oil-spice mixture on the roast (if desired, stuff into the middle of the cut). It is beneficial to use a bowl that is so small that there is almost no room between the roast and the wall of the bowl.

The roast has to marinate in the refrigerator for one to two days. It should be carefully rotated every four to six hours so the oil redistributes itself.

For cooking, the meat is simply placed in the Dutch oven and cooked. Oil is not needed since the meat still contains enough oil from the marinating. Before putting the lid on top, you have to add a quarter cup of water per pound of meat, so the roast doesn't burn. You can also distribute fresh onion pieces on top.

The two pounds (1kg) of meat requires one hour to be done. For the second two pounds count on 45 minutes. For every additional two pounds, add another 30 minutes. So a six pound (3kg) roast has to cook for two hours and 15 minutes. However, a roast should not exceed six pounds, so it is better to divide larger roasts.

Sprinkle the marinated roast with onions, place it into the Dutch oven and add a bit of water.

Piled on top of each other, you can simultaneously prepare two dishes.

The finished rotisserie roast is juicy and the accompanying sauce is delicious!

Boiled Beef Brisket

INGREDIENTS FOR 6 PERSONS

- 3 lbs (1.5kg) beef brisket
- 1 jar horseradish
- 1 carrot
- 2 onions
- 1 cup raisins
- 1 pint (1/2l) beer
- pepper and salt

Beef brisket has to cook a long time to become truly tender. On the other hand, this meat is cheaper to buy. For the long cooking time the Dutch oven is well suited, since you can cook in it for a long time at low temperatures. However, you can also use a kettle that you hang over a campfire if you can guarantee that the heat can be kept constant over such a long timespan. If you don't own a Dutch oven, you can let the dish simmer in a standard pot too; for this, place the pot by the fire for a longer period of time.

Salt and pepper the beef brisket and rub it with horseradish. Place it into the Dutch oven or into a pot. Cut the carrot and the onions into coarse cubes, then add to the meat along with the raisins. Fill up the whole thing with beer and let it simmer for a few hours. The dish has to cook for at least three hours, otherwise the beef brisket won't be tender. Occasionally, you should look into the pot and replace any evaporated liquid with water.

At the end of the cooking time the sauce is nice and thick. The spiciness of the horseradish and the sweet raisins provide the special taste of this dish.

Boiled potatoes and beans cooked in a bottle (see page 72) taste good with beef brisket. A fitting beverage is beer.

Quick Roast

Especially when cooking outdoors, you want to have a presentable result with as little effort as possible. That is the case with this roast. The preparation is easy, but, unfortunately, it takes a long time to cook.

Pour a good shot of olive oil into the Dutch oven and put the salted and peppered roast on top. Put the bacon strips on top of the roast, then add the onions and one cup water. With plenty of top heat, the first two pounds of meat cook in two hours; for each additional two pounds add an extra hour.

Check every once in a while and occasionally add water, so the roast does not burn. Before serving, let the roast sit a bit. Bring the broth to a boil and thicken it to taste with flour.

> **INGREDIENTS PER PERSONS**
>
> - 10–14 oz (300–400g) roast
> - 1 onion
> - bacon strips to put on top
> - pepper and salt

Cover the roast with bacon strips and onions.

Add water when needed.

Baeckeoffe

INGREDIENTS FOR ABOUT 6-8 PERSONS

- 1-1/2 lb (750g) pork shoulder
- 1-1/2 lb (750g) beef brisket
- 1-1/2 lb (750g) lamb shoulder without bones
- 1 pork hock and 1 pig's tail (if desired)
- 3 large onions
- 2 sticks of leek
- 5 garlic cloves
- 2 laurel leaves
- 2 crushed cloves
- 3 lbs (1.5kg) potatoes
- 1 bottle Alsace Riesling
- pepper and salt
- 1 teaspoon thyme
- 1 teaspoon marjoram
- a bit of rosemary

Baeckeoffe is a former army dish from the Alsace. This dish was prepared by the women on a laundry day and baked for 3–4 hours in the baker's oven in a casserole dish with lid. Here we prepare it at the campfire in a cast iron pot.

Cut the meat into bite-sized cubes, deeply score the pork hock and pig's tail at several places, and salt and pepper everything. Then prepare a marinade using the white wine, the finely chopped garlic cloves, the laurel leaves, cloves, thyme, marjoram, and the twig of rosemary.

The next day, peel the potatoes and cut them into slices. Place a layer of potato slices and a bit of coarsely chopped leek and onions into the cast iron pot. Add the meat and the pork hock with additional finely chopped onions. Put the remaining potato slices, onion, and leek pieces on top of the meat. Pour the marinade over it. If necessary, add some water until the cast iron pot is filled 3/4 of the way. Now the dish is cooked at low heat by the side of the fire for at least two-and-a-half or, preferably, three-and-a-half to four hours.

You must not marinate the meat in a cast iron pot since it would immediately rust.

Layer the ingredients in the cast iron pot.

The pot sits next to the fire for several hours.

The longer the dish simmers, the better it tastes.

Chicken Curry in the Potjie

Of course, this dish also
works in the Dutch oven

The Boers in South Africa cook at the campfire with the potjie (pronounced poy-key). There are two standard dishes. For one there is the Potjie-Kos, which means food from the potjie. This is a stew similar to goulash, which simmers in the potjie for a long time. Due to the round bottom the liquid collects at the deepest point in the pot and the dish can hardly burn. Due to the special shape of the lid the evaporated liquid drips back into the food. The legs are a bit longer than those of the Dutch oven, which is because the potjie is heated with fire and you need a bit more distance above the ground for that than for cooking with embers.

The ingredients are browned one after the other.

Then the entire thing is filled up with coconut milk ...

... and has to simmer for some time in the embers.

The curry is spicy, but has a pleasant taste.

Cut the chicken into small pieces, the vegetables into small cubes, and the leeks into rings. Heat heavily underneath the potjie with wood as thick as a thumb. In the potjie, the individual ingredients are browned one after the other. Have a bowl with the cut ingredients ready and an empty bowl for the browned ingredients. Pour half a cup oil into the pot and brown the chicken in it, one serving at a time, until it is nice and brown all the way around. Then remove it with a skimmer and place it into the empty bowl. One after the other, brown all chicken parts and then dust them in the bowl with curry powder. By and by, brown the vegetables and also place them into the bowl. If needed, add some oil. Once everything has been browned, put the pineapple pieces and the coconut milk, along with all the browned ingredients, into the pot and carefully stir it once. Season with harissa or sambal oelek, salt and pepper. The liquid should barely cover the vegetables. Now you should merely allow the dish to simmer for two hours with few embers or in the heat radiating from the fire. On burning wood pieces, as when browning, the heat is much too strong for simmering and the food will inevitably burn.

Traditionally this dish is eaten with corn porridge (a type of polenta) made of cornmeal, but rice also tastes good with it.

Melie-Pap (Corn Porridge)

Put the cold water, the crumbled broth cube, and the salt into a potjie. Then pour the flour all at once into the cold water and beat it heavily with a whisk until no more lumps are visible. Place the pot on the fire and bring the water to a boil while continuing to stir with the whisk. By and by, the flour will bubble up and the porridge will solidify. Then use a wooden spoon. If the dish becomes too solid, then thin it with some water. If it is too liquid, then add some flour. Shortly before serving, add butter to taste.

The real Melie-Pap has nothing to do with the yellow cornmeal for polenta. Even though Melie-Pap is also made from corn, it is peeled before grinding and is white. For barbecue events Pap is prepared much drier so it can absorb the sauce.

Tip:

The mix ratio of one cup flour and two cups of water always works!

INGREDIENTS FOR 6-8 PERSONS

- 1 chicken (3 lbs/1.4 kg) or chicken drumsticks
- 3 large onions
- 2 garlic cloves
- 2 carrots
- 1 kohlrabi
- 1 eggplant
- 1/2 lb (250g) mushrooms
- 1/2 celery knob
- 1–2 sticks leek
- 2 bell peppers
- 3-1/2 cups (800ml) coconut milk
- 1 can pineapple pieces with juice
- pepper and salt
- plenty of curry powder (at least 3 tablespoons)
- harissa or sambal-olek
- oil for frying
- possibly fresh ginger and lemon grass

INGREDIENTS FOR 6-8 PERSONS

- 1-1/2 qts (1.5l) water
- 1 lb (500g) cornmeal (fine as powder), preferably the real Melie-Pap made of white flour
- salt
- 1 broth cube
- butter

Kale Hike

In winter, when the parish lands are frozen and snowed in, it is time for us in Northern Germany to go on the traditional kale hikes. Kale is a really fabulous winter vegetable, but it must have been exposed to frost for it not to be bitter.

To prepare a hearty meal over the open fire for these hikes, you need a large pan for the fried potatoes and a kettle or a Dutch oven for the kale, for which the Dutch oven works particularly well. Light a fire and, once the fire has burned down, set the Dutch oven (filled according to the preparation directions) into it. Now you can hike for two hours, as is the custom. When you return you just need to fry the prepared potatoes and, after 15 minutes, everyone has a hot meal on their plate: Kale, tea sausage, Bregen sausage, bacon, pork belly, smoked pork chop, and fried potatoes. Serve corn schnapps with this, one beforehand, one during the meal, and one afterward.

Bregen sausage is sausage consisting of fat, rind, and grout, which can really be found only in Northern Germany. Instead of this sausage you can also use the ends of tea sausages.

Kale with Bregen Sausage and Meat

Put one tablespoon of lard into the Dutch oven. Brown the diced onions in it, then add the kale and fill it up with the broth (so it isn't too dry and burns), then salt and pepper. Crumble the Bregen sausage from the can over the kale and mix it in. Add the mettwurst and the meat slices to the kale. Let the pot sit in the hot embers with low top heat. Remember: "Kale has to glow like a freshly harvested clod!"

If desired, you can also prepare this dish with Sauerkraut.

INGREDIENTS FOR 2 PERSONS

- 1 tablespoon lard
- 2 tablespoons onion cubes
- 1 can kale
- 1 cup (250ml) broth from soup cubes
- 1 can loose bregen sausage
- 1 mettwurst
- 1 slice pork belly
- 1 slice smoked pork chop
- 1 slice smoked bacon

Sweet Fried Potatoes

The cast iron pan stores a lot of heat, so you should remove it from the fire for caramelizing.

To go with the kale we serve a specialty: sweet fried potatoes. That sounds funny at first, but once you have tasted it, you will want it over and over again.

The night before, cook unpeeled potatoes that are about the size of plums and let them cool. The next day the potatoes are peeled and are then already "greasy." Take a large iron or cast iron pan and heat lard or clarified butter. Put the potatoes in whole. As soon as they are nicely brown and crispy all around, sprinkle sugar on the potatoes and let it caramelize so that it loses its sweetness. You have to make sure that it doesn't caramelize too much and become bitter.

BAKING
AT THE FIRE

Rolls and Cinnamon Buns

INGREDIENTS FOR ONE 14" DUTCH OVEN (10–12 ROLLS)

- 6 cups (750g) flour
- 2 bags dry yeast
- 1/2 cup warm water or milk
- 2 tablespoons oil
- 1 teaspoon Salt
- 1/2 teaspoon Sugar

INGREDIENTS FOR ONE 14" DUTCH OVEN (10–12 PIECES)

Dough:

- 7 cups flour
- 2 teaspoons salt
- 1/2 cup sugar
- 2 packets dry yeast
- 2 cups warm milk
- 4 eggs
- 2 tablespoons shortening

Filling:

- 2 tablespoons melted butter
- 1 teaspoon cinnamon brown sugar
- 1 tablespoon cocoa powder

Yeast Rolls

Mix the ingredients for the basic dough well and knead, then cover it in a pot with a towel and put it in a room-temperature location for half an hour so the yeast dough can rise. The prepared dough is then divided into 10–12 equal balls that are individually dusted with flour so they don't stick together while baking.

Now place the dough balls into the Dutch oven with some distance between them. Let them rise again until they have doubled in size, then place the Dutch oven on the embers. Experience tells us that 30–40 minutes are enough if the charcoal is already glowing nicely. Test them with a toothpick. When they are baked, no dough will stick to the wood when you poke the toothpick in and pull it out again.

Cinnamon Buns

Mix all the ingredients for the dough until it separates from the bowl and is solid and malleable. Then let the dough rise for an hour until it has doubled in height.

Roll out the dough and spread the filling. Then roll the dough up and cut slices that are placed next to each other in the greased Dutch oven. The dough has to rise once again until it has again doubled in height.

With just a little heat underneath the Dutch oven and a lot of heat on the lid, the cinnamon buns are baked to a golden yellow color in 30–40 minutes.

With the beans serve yeast rolls (1), and, as dessert, cinnamon buns (2), and Pineapple Upside Down Cake (3).

Pineapple Upside Down Cake

Dessert can also be prepared in a Dutch oven. A simple recipe is the pineapple upside down cake. The fruit is placed on the bottom of the pot and covered with the dough. After baking the cake is turned upside down, which is where the name comes from. If you want to make the dessert particularly appetizing, place a red cocktail cherry into the center of each slice of pineapple.

You can also use a bake mix, but you have to omit half the eggs so the dough doesn't rise too much.

Line the Dutch oven with a double layer of aluminum foil. Place the pot on the fire and melt the butter in the aluminum foil. Sprinkle the sugar on top and spread the fruit, but without its liquid. Then spoon the mixed dough over the fruit such that it is uniformly distributed.

Close the lid and heat the Dutch oven with a little bottom heat and a lot of top heat. After 20 minutes, the cake should be done. Open the lid and test it with a toothpick or thin wooden stick.

You should bake the cake to a golden brown and then let it cool a bit in the Dutch oven. Carefully lift the cake out of the pot using the overhanging aluminum foil. Don't damage the aluminum foil while doing this.

Now you just have to turn the cake upside down. For this, the bottom (which is still on top right now!) is covered with a plate, a second plate is placed under the cake, and both plates are rotated 180 degrees so that the bottom one ends up on top. Then pull off the aluminum foil—and enjoy!

INGREDIENTS FOR A 10"-DUTCH OVEN

- 1 can (425 ml) pineapple in slices
- 1 teaspoon butter
- 2 tablespoon sugar

Dough:
- 1 cup wheat flour
- 1 cup cornmeal
- 1 egg
- 1 pinch of salt
- 1 tablespoon sugar
- 1 teaspoon baking powder
  milk (amount based on need, so that you get a viscous mass)

Sourdough Rye Rolls

Rye rolls with sourdough are more wholesome over the long run.

You can also bake real bread in a Dutch oven. However, it is easier and more convenient to bake sourdough rolls that taste delicious.

The sourdough for these rolls is made exclusively with rye flour. During baking, wheat flour is added to encourage positive baking behavior. Sourdough rye rolls, the daily bread of the trappers and cowboys in America, were traditionally baked in a Dutch oven.

The old trappers could make sourdough out in the wild. They mixed the dough with flour until it was dry and crumbly, then it was placed into the pant pockets, wrapped in a cloth so it wouldn't freeze.

Prepare the pre-dough the previous evening: Move the sourdough (about two cups) into a larger bowl and mix a thick dough together with two cups rye flour and lukewarm water. Let it sit overnight, wrapped in a towel, at a warm location.

The next day, mix the dry yeast with wheat flour, salt, and sugar in a bowl, add two cups of sourdough from the previous day, and knead it to a dough that no longer sticks to the bowl or the fingers with water (or buttermilk). Shape the dough into a lump and let it rise in the bowl for an hour until the mass has doubled. By the campfire the dough is placed into the Dutch oven and left to rise for an hour with a few embers on the lid.

If the dough has doubled, then it is kneaded into a roll, but not too hard, so the air bubbles remain in the dough. Using a knife, cut the dough into ten fairly uniform rolls, which are then placed in a circle in the Dutch oven. The cut pieces of dough must not be kneaded again since they don't rise well due to the rye. They are dusted with plenty of flour, put in the Dutch oven and again heated for an hour with a little glowing coal on the lid, so they can rise a second time. For baking, 1/4 to 1/3 of the embers is distributed underneath the Dutch oven and the rest on the lid. After about 20 minutes, the rolls are done.

Don't bake bannock too fast. It will burn before it can rise.

Bannock is always torn, never cut since that brings bad luck.

Bannock

Bannock is the bread of the wilderness and is always prepared by the open fire. Prepare dense dough that is easily removed from the bowl with flour, water, salt, grease, and baking powder. Knead well with your hands for three minutes and shape into a flat loaf, about 1/4-inch thick. Heat grease in the pan and bake the bannock golden brown on both sides. Bannock tastes best warm and fresh.

Better than the common bannock is sourdough bannock. For this, use one cup flour less than for the common one, but add a cup sourdough.

If you bake bannock more frequently, get some sourdough starter at the bakery and mix it with one cup water and two tablespoons of flour at home. After two days in a warm location, the sourdough is bubbly and ready for use. Replace the amount you use with water and flour. Sourdough starter should be as fluid as pancake dough.

INGREDIENTS PER PERSON

- 2 cups flour
- 1 teaspoon baking powder
- 1/2 teaspoon salt
- 1 tablespoon grease or oil
- water
- grease for baking

Drying sourdough is no problem if you don't wish to bake for a while

A delicacy is hiding under this crust!

Peach Cobbler

A "cobbler" is a true Dutch oven dessert. Incredibly easy to make, it is a hit with children and anyone with a sweet tooth. Cobbler is served warm out of the Dutch oven with peach liqueur (of course only for adults) and vanilla ice cream. The advantage of this recipe is that you can easily prepare the items outdoors. For practice use a scale to begin with and weigh the ingredients as you add them one by one.

Put the flour, sugar, salt, and baking powder into a bowl. On the side melt the butter in a metal bowl by the campfire and heat the milk. With a whisk beat the butter and milk into the dry ingredients. The dough should be as fluid as waffle dough.

Pour one can of fruit with syrup and the remaining peaches without syrup into the Dutch oven. Then pour the dough in an even layer on top of the fruit and sprinkle with the brown sugar and the butter flakes. Bake with little bottom heat until the fruit comes to a boil, then continue baking with top heat until the top has a brown crust.

INGREDIENTS FOR A 12" DUTCH OVEN (4–6 PERSONS)

- 2 large cans peaches
- 2-1/2 cups (300g) flour
- 3/4 cup (50g) sugar
- 1/2 teaspoon salt
- 3 teaspoons baking powder
- 1 cup (250ml) milk or buttermilk
- 1/2 cup (150g) melted butter
- brownbugar
- butter flakes

First place the fruit into the Dutch oven.

Then pour the dough onto the fruit in a uniform layer.

Sprinkle plenty of brown sugar onto the dough.

Butter flakes are the finishing touch.

Bread that Turns Out

Get a bread mix of your choice (ciabatta or rye bread with yeast is well suited). They tend to be sold in 1-pound (500g) packages. Prepare a package according to the directions and let it rise for 30 minutes in the bowl. Then briefly knead the dough with flour-covered hands on a floured surface (in order not to disturb the already formed bubbles in the dough) and form a roll. Cut it crosswise with a knife into two equally long pieces. These are again cut and recut again into two pieces each time so that you end up with eight almost uniform pieces of dough. These are shaped into balls without much kneading.

INGREDIENTS FOR 1 LOAF OF BREAD

- 1 lb (500g) bread mix
- flour for working
- grease for the Dutch oven

In this photo you can see that you can, of course, put more than 8 pieces of dough in the Dutch oven in an arbitrary order.

To prepare the 12" Dutch oven for baking, grease the bottom and the wall and flour the bottom. Place the first dough ball in the middle and the other seven at regular intervals around it. The balls should not touch each other.

To let the dough rise the second time, put the lid on and place four glowing pieces of coal on the lid. This usually has to rise another 30–40 minutes, and, during this time, you should rotate the lid every few minutes to radiate the warmth, not the heat, uniformly.

To bake the bread, heat the Dutch oven for 15 minutes, with nine pieces of coal below and fifteen pieces of coal on the lid. Then move four coals from below to the lid for another 15 minutes. After that the bread should be ready for the first bake test. The bread should have a golden yellow to dark brown surface, depending on the variety. Poke through the bread with a long fork or knitting needle from top to bottom. By doing this, you will feel the thickness of the crust, the consistency of the dough, and the thickness of the bottom, which has a tendency to burn. The bread is done baking when you pull the knitting needle out and there are no pieces of dough stuck to it, and when you knock on the bread it has to sound hollow. The finished bread is easy to lift out of the Dutch oven and should be cooled on a grate.

Wood Baking Oven

General Remarks about the Wood Baking Oven

There are two varieties of wood oven: in one variety the baking area and the fire chamber are separate, and in the other the fire is started in a single chamber where the baking also takes place. For the cake flambé, a variation with little room for the fire is used. This way you can continuously bake cake flambé or pizza.

Cake Flambé

Cake flambé is a specialty from the Alsace that consists of a very thin bottom that can be purchased already baked. First, season crème fraîche generously with pepper, salt, and ground nutmeg, and stir thoroughly. Roll out the dough to the thickness of the back of a knife, dust with plenty of flour, spread the crème fraîche mixture, and cover with finely cut bacon, Emmentaler cheese, and onions.

The cake bakes by the heat from the stone, while the toppings bake because of the flames that lap over the cake flambé from the sides. Place the cake into the baking chamber, then close all doors and wait a minute. When the bottom is done, it puffs up. Then open the bottom door, causing the flames to sweep over the toppings from three sides and melt the cheese. With a well-practiced team of two helpers you can comfortably bake 30 to 40 cakes flambé in an hour.

Only use dry beech wood, about as thick as two fingers. It will burn fast and doesn't smoke much. The temperature should be about 650–750° F (350–400° C). If the temperature rises too high and the bottoms of the Cakes Flambé turn black, cool the firebricks with a wet rag or half a glass of water. You can pour the water onto the hot stones—they can take it.

If you wish to prepare the dough yourself, use the recipe for pizza dough (p. 119).

INGREDIENTS FOR THE TOPPING PER SMALL CAKE FLAMBÉ (SURFACE ABOUT 8" X 10")

- 1 lb premade dough
- 1/4 cup (40g) crème fraîche
- 1 slice (30g) bacon
- 1/4 cup (30g) Emmentaler cheese
- 1/3 cup (40g) onions
- pepper and salt
- nutmeg
- flour for working

For separating, use a long knife that you push down onto the cutting surface.

Pizza

For a proper pizza, the bottom is the decisive element, and for that the proper choice of flour must be made. You need type 550, not type 405, which is suitable for cake flour. The second important ingredient is time. Good pizza dough takes time.

Sieve the flour into a bowl and make an indentation in the middle. Into this indentation put the crumbled yeast, the sugar, and the water. Knead well and let it rise, covered, for half an hour at a warm location. Then add salt and olive oil and knead heavily. Then the dough has to rise again at a warm location for an hour. Another possibility is cool fermentation, where the dough takes four to six hours to rise properly either in the refrigerator or at room temperature. It turns out considerably better this way than with the fast method at a warm location.

And now for the topping: Good pizza should not be topped with watery items. This is where most mistakes are made. A pizza has a thin and crispy bottom. Then you add a thin layer of tomato sauce, then the cheese, and on top of that go the other ingredients. The cheese does not belong over everything. That is a widespread misconception. Fully baked pizza dough is like crisp bread.

Knead the risen dough one more time and shape into balls the size of an apples. Roll them out and fold them up slightly at the edges so the toppings do not run under the dough.

The dough bakes by the heat of the stone; when it is brown on the bottom the pizza is done. If a greedy person has put double or triple the toppings on the pizza and it soaks the bottom, the pizza cannot be saved. Covered excessively it's a vegetable cake or a quiche.

First season the tomato sauce, made of pureed tomatoes out of the can (pizza tomatoes), with oregano and pepper; spread it thinly (!) over the dough. Then sprinkle all topping ingredients except for the fresh mushrooms and the salami (these go on top of the cheese), as well as plenty of oregano on top. Follow this with the cheese, the mushrooms, and the salami.

The pizza oven should be significantly hotter than 650° F (350° C) to be at operating temperature. This difference to the 450° C (230° C) of the home baking oven makes the difference in taste. The pizza is done baking when the edge of the dough is light brown and no longer bends over. You are baking the dough with the heat from the stone and, if you wish to check how far along the dough is, then you can tell from its underside. Briefly open the bottom door, and the flames will flicker over the pizza and bake the toppings.

> **Tip:**
>
> For the pizza or the cake flambé to easily slide off the spatula, sprinkle some polenta (cornmeal) onto the spatula. The semolina acts like a ball bearing and the pizza easily slides from the board onto the firebrick.

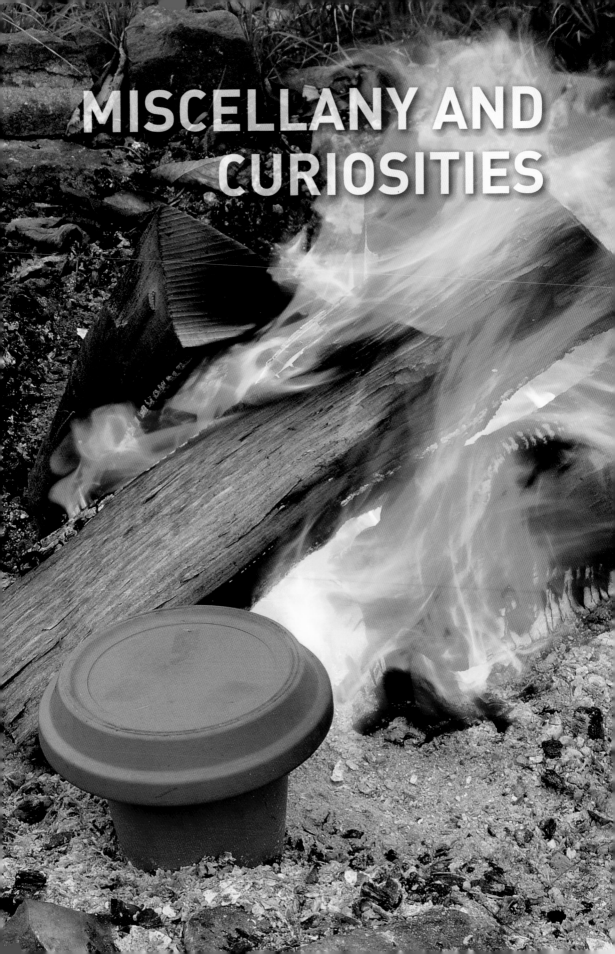

MISCELLANY AND
CURIOSITIES

Turkey in the Can

INGREDIENTS PER PERSON

- 1 lb (500g) turkey
- salt and pepper to taste
- poultry spices

The traditional dish for Thanksgiving in America is turkey, which, due to its size, is a challenge for every homemaker, since it fits into almost no oven. If you roast your turkey by the open fire, you don't have that problem, since there is a simple trick: build yourself an oven out of a large pot and heat with grilling briquettes.

This can be done using a large metal trash can, which can be found at most hardware stores (since these are not available here in Germany, we have used a large stew pot). You can also use cut, 8- or 12-gallon (30 to 50 liter) beer barrels made of stainless steel that you can get at little cost from a scrap metal dealer. There are two ways to support the turkey. The easiest method is to line the ground with aluminum foil and drive a stake in the middle. The turkey is placed on the stake (you can also use a commercially available metal turkey or chicken holder instead). Alternatively, the turkey can be supported into a low pot, so that the breast faces up and can turn nice and brown. You have to set this pot on one or two bricks.

When the turkey is positioned, the large trash can or pot is inverted over the turkey and pushed slightly into the ground; this forms the oven. The oven is heated with two 8-lb sacks of charcoal briquettes, spread on the top and at the bottom edge. After roughly an hour, the embers must be refreshed by adding additional pieces of charcoal. After one-and-a-half to two hours, the turkey is so tender that the meat falls off the bones.

The seasoned tom turkey is placed on a chicken holder and set on the aluminum foil.

A row of glowing, grilling briquettes is placed around the bottom edge and one load on top of the pot.

After about 2 hours, the turkey is coooked.

Original Peka from Hungary

In the land of the Magyars, cooking by the campfire is traditional. Much less well known than the goulash kettles are the baking domes called Peka.

These are offered by many small companies in greatly varying versions and sizes, from simple clay or tin versions to the cast iron pekas with enamel on the inside.

With a diameter of about 20 inches (50cm), the peka is ideal for the cozy evening in a circle of eight to twelve people. The base has three short legs and a low rim so that the meat or fish can be removed more easily. The lid, more properly a dome, is enameled on the inside as well and has a "crown" so that the piled-on embers don't fall off. The enameling is very important because this large peka cannot simply be put into a standard sink for washing. It is too large and heavy for that. You can clean the peka outdoors directly by the fire with a sponge and hot water. The exterior is merely brushed off.

Traditionally you heat the peka with embers from a wood fire, not with charcoal briquettes as with the Dutch ovens. To prevent the relatively heavy pekas from sinking into the ground, you line the fire place with bricks. You start a fire next to the peka and remove its embers for cooking.

In the remote areas of Hungary, the peka is still used today to bake bread and cake. Additionally, it lends itself to dishes where the meat or fish is cooked together with the accompaniments, such as vegetables or potatoes.

For example, lamb with fresh green beans and lots of garlic. Even a fawn can be cooked without a problem, when cut into pieces. There is more than enough room for that or a goose or duck on red cabbage, a roasting chicken on potatoes, onions and bell pepper strips, salmon on a bed of vegetables, an entire pork shoulder as a pork roast with crackling, crispy pork legs, or pot roast. Particularly impressive is a whole, cooked octopus. The operation is very simple: First the vegetables, such as potatoes and onions, are placed in the peka. Don't forget plenty of garlic. Then the meat or fish is added, followed by the herbs and spices. Fill the whole thing with water or wine. Then cover with the dome and cook the dish for two hours with very few embers from below and lots of heat from above.

Resist the temptation to check every ten minutes to see "whether something is happening yet." When the two hours has passed, take the dome off and place the bottom directly onto the table. The stored heat keeps the food hot for a surprisingly long time.

A peka is a "baking dome" with a lid that has a "crown," on which embers are piled.

There are numerous dishes that can be easily prepared in a Peka. You can even bake in it.

Lamb Shoulder with Various Beans

Line the peka with the beans and the cut up vegetables, then spike the lamb quarter with garlic and set it into the middle of the Peka. Add the various beans around the lamb. Season with plenty of savory spices, as well as salt and pepper. Place the peka onto just a few embers and cover with the hood; cover with embers. Every half an hour add fresh embers onto the hood. Depending on the size of the piece of meat, roast it for 1-1/2 to 2 hours.

INGREDIENTS FOR ABOUT 10 PERSONS

- 1 lamb front quarter
- various beans (broad or fava beans and white beans out of the can, fresh green beans, and string beans)
- plenty of garlic
- vegetables in season (potatoes, onions, bell peppers, tomatoes, mushrooms, etc.)
- pepper and salt
- savory spices

The Peka sits on the left; the fire burns to the right to produce embers.

Distribute the vegetables in the bowl below and place the meat in the middle.

The dish has to cook like this for at least two hours.

The meat is so tender that it falls off the bones.

Goose in the Earth Oven

INGREDIENTS FOR 4 PERSONS

- 1 wild or domestic goose
- 2 cans red cabbage
- 1 sour apple
- pepper and salt

The earth oven must be heated for at least three hours. When closing it, it is important that the oven is airtight since the embers will keep glowing otherwise, which makes it much too hot.

The earth oven is not a recipe, but a type of preparation. This type of cooking was made famous by German forces in the African colony that is now Namibia, in the years before World War I. Salted and peppered poultry or game (guinea fowl and kudu meat) are placed in a roaster together with onions and potatoes as well as root vegetables. The meat and vegetables should basically fill up the pot. The gaps are filled up halfway with water. Then the pot is lowered into an earth oven.

An earth oven is very easy to build: You dig a hole into the ground that is three times as deep as the pot is high and offers space about the width of a hand all around the pot. You maintain a fire in it for about three hours, until plenty of embers are available. With a shovel lift out about half of the embers, put the pot inside, and cover it with the removed embers. Then cover the hole with the removed dirt and leave it alone for four to six hours. When the food is done, the hole is reopened and the pot is lifted out.

The dish can also be cooked in an old goose roaster. These do not, however, seal as tightly as Dutch ovens and sand and ashes can get into the food, so you should cover such a pot with aluminum foil.

For this type of preparation older game is also suitable because even this tougher, gamier meat will turn tender and tasty due to the long cooking time. In some regions you can use deer meat, wild boar, or red deer meat.

You can use game or poultry or both. For this recipe we will use a goose. First pepper and salt the goose and stuff it with the apple. Put the red cabbage into the roaster and place the goose on top. You have to cook the goose and red cabbage at least three hours in the earth oven. The fat that runs from the bird gives the red cabbage its inimitable taste.

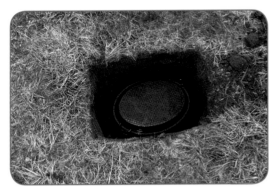

First excavate the hole and set the roaster in it to check the depth and diameter.

Maintain a strong fire in the hole for two hours.

Place the meat on the vegetables. Here is the goose on top of the red cabbage.

Lower the roaster into the embers.

The grass sod has to cover the hole again and the edges must be sealed airtight.

After a few hours the food is done.

Pork in the Earth Oven

INGREDIENTS PER PERSON

- 2 lbs (1 kg) suckling pig
- 1 onion
- fresh kitchen herbs
- pepper and palt

For suckling pigs a weight over 15 kg stops being interesting for beginners. You should definitely not use a heavier suckling pig for this type of preparation since the legs have a hard time getting done.

Building a real earth oven is a rather sweaty chore. First, a sufficiently large hole has to be excavated; then, three times the amount of wood that fits into the hole has to be burned in it to produce enough heat. Place several baseball-sized rocks onto the fire, so these can be heated as well. These are later put on top of the pork.

The suckling pig should be stuffed with onions and herbs. To prevent the meat from picking up an unwanted flavor, you should not use twigs from coniferous woods as cover. The pork rests on plenty of twigs, with which it is is also covered. Then the heated rocks and the excavated grass sod and dirt are placed on top until you don't see any more smoke.

A disadvantage of the earth oven is that you can't "take a look" in between. Therefore, you should be prepared to finish roasting a few sections that didn't quite fully cook on the grill or in a pan. Especially in the summer, this is definitely necessary with pork.

In order to make it easier to put the pork into the hole or take it out, a wire mesh (without plastic!) is made out of four long wires to suspend the pork as if in a hammock.

It needs to be said that guests always have the expectation of a "crispy crust" with a suckling pig, but that isn't the case with pork from the earth oven. So this can easily lead to disappointment.

The suckling pig is stuffed with onions and fresh herbs, and the earth oven is heated until triple the amount of wood has burned off.

You insulate the pork with a lot of green material...

...then cover the hole for at least eight hours.

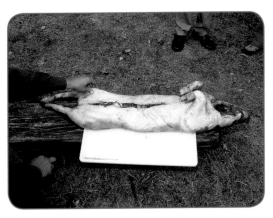

After digging it out and rinsing it, the suckling pig is ready to be eaten.

Chicken in a "Clay Coat"

Obtaining the proper clay with a consistency suitable for this recipe is not easy, so we use a salt dough that is very easy to prepare. One part salt is combined with four parts flour (by measure; 1 to 2 parts by weight) and as much water as needed to make dough that doesn't stick to the hands. This dough is rolled out and wrapped around the chicken, then the edges are kneaded together. The coat, about 1/2-inch thick, should be completely sealed so the chicken can cook in its own juices.

With your hands, carefully loosen the skin from the breast, back, and the drumsticks, and push the stuffing, consisting of spices, herbs, lemon peel, butter, salt, garlic, fine onion cubes, and lemon juice, together with the lemon slices under the skin of the chicken. The squeezed lemon is put directly into the chest cavity. Knead a dense dough out of the dough ingredients and wrap the chicken in it. After three hours in the embers, the chicken is done. When opening the cover you should wear thick gloves since the escaping steam is very hot. Alternatively, you can use clay or loam, but then the "coat" is as hard as stone and you will need a hammer.

Be careful when opening because a lot of hot steam escapes that could scald you.

INGREDIENTS FOR 4 PERSONS

- 1 roasting chicken (about 3-1/2 lbs [1,500g])

Stuffing:
- 1 lemon, sliced
- 1 lemon, peel grated off, pressed,
- 1 tablespoon butter
- 1 onion, diced
- pepper and salt
- 1 garlic clove, pressed
- plenty of kitchen herbs (parsley, marjoram, thyme)

Dough:
- 8 cups (1kg) flour
- 2 cups (500g) salt
- water

The lemon slices and the rest of the stuffing go under the skin.

Wrap the chicken in the dough.

The package which is sealed all the way around, is placed on the embers.

Carefully rotate the package until it turns hard everywhere.

The finished package is not very attractive…

… but the contents taste extremely good.

The reflector oven folded up and put together.

Reflector Oven

A light-weight alternative to the Dutch oven for baking and scalloping is the reflector oven. It is unfolded, placed next to the blazing fire and reflects the heat rays from the fire from above and below onto the food in the middle on the two supports. Despite the fairly uniform heat from above and below, the side of the dish facing the fire is subject to significantly more heat. Therefore you need to regularly rotate the food, so it doesn't burn on one side. The reflector oven is not just good for scalloping, but was once also used for both roasting meat and baking bread in the house as well.

Spaghetti with Cheese

This is a good dish to practice with the reflector oven and to use up leftovers.

Put the spaghetti into a fireproof dish that fits into the reflector oven. Beat the eggs with the ham and onion cubes, season with salt and pepper, and pour the mixture over the spaghetti. On top of that sprinkle the shredded cheese. Then scallop the whole thing in the reflector oven until the egg mixture has set and the cheese has melted.

INGREDIENTS

- boiled spaghetti
- diced ham
- diced onions
- eggs
- pepper and salt
- shredded Cheese

Since this is a recipe for the use of leftovers, there are no precise quantities listed here. Simply use what is available.

You regulate the heat in the oven by changing the distance to the fire.

Caramel by the Campfire

Frequently you need an easy-to-prepare sauce for your dessert. There is a very easy solution for this: sweetened Russian condensed milk. You can get these cans in many supermarkets or in Russian specialty stores. If you cannot find it, sweetened domestic condensed milk can be substituted.

Cook one can of sweetened condensed milk in a pot of water by the campfire for two hours. Leave the can unopened. During this long cooking, the contents will caramelize and become thick. It is important to stick to the two-hour timespan; one hour is not enough. Also, the water has to remain at a rolling boil and not just simmer. After the two hours, you can open the can and remove the contents.

It is simply a delight with fresh waffles, pancakes, ice cream, or baked apples!

Place the unopened can into a pot of water.

The contents have to cook for at least two hours next to the fire.

After two hours the caramel is done.

Open the can carefully.

Baked Apple in a Clay Pot

You need a clay pot with saucer, an apple, honey, and marzipan.

Baked apples are a treat that has fallen into oblivion for no good reason. Yet they are so easy to make. You only need a clay flower pot (without a hole) and a matching saucer. The apple is prepared by simply cutting the core out with a corer. Into this hole you can place the various mixtures, but, as is often the case in life, the simplest is also the tastiest. So either take marzipan paste or a marzipan potato and knead it so it fits into the hole in the apple, then put a half teaspoon of honey on the apple. Put the apple into the flower pot and cover the pot with the saucer. After ten minutes in the hot ashes next to the fire, the apple should be done. You can tell because the apple will get runny.

Baked apples go well with vanilla sauce, vanilla ice cream or the caramel sauce from page 133.

Put the apple into the pot, place it by the fire, and cover it with the saucer.

It is a wonderful treat with caramel sauce.

FIELD KITCHEN RECIPES

Fifteen gallons of pea soup in the pot.

Specialties of the Field Kitchen

Cooking for many people by the open fire and in the field kitchen presents particularly high demands on the campfire cook. Starting with the selection of the recipes, you have to take into consideration the limited options when cooking. For providing for about 50 people—the most an average cook can handle—you need a kettle that can hold at least 7-1/2 gallons (30 liters). Just handling out the servings to 50 people takes about half an hour, so for more people a second disbursement station needs to be established. Also, a pot with 6 or 7 gallons of hot pea soup cannot be safely moved by one person alone.

Count on 1-3/4 cups (400ml) soup per person; for hungry hunters or hikers you may need to count on about 3 cups (750ml). From an 8-gallon kettle that can only be filled with 6 or 7 gallons, you thus obtain about 37 to 64 meals. If you want to fortify the soup with sausage, slice the sausage so it can be eaten more easily.

To bring a pot with 25 liters of water to a boil you need at least half an hour. You should heat the kettle with grilling briquettes or charcoal; this is very clean and provides uniform heat over a longer period of time as is necessary for cooking soups. If you have a camp stove with gas fuel, you can place it under it even if that isn't really the proper style. To change the height between the pot and the fire, place the legs of the tripod closer to the fire or farther away. This way the kettle hangs higher or lower. Extending the chain is hardly possible since the kettle, weighing over 65 pounds, can hardly be moved while over the fire. You should definitely use a kettle hook with which you can move the kettle easily and safely, even when full.

If you intend to be a campfire cook more frequently, you can make your guests happy and not serve the food on plastic or paper plates, but on enameled tin plates that are easier to hold in your hand as well. If you also use normal spoons, eating outdoors becomes a real treat.

When you test a large kettle for the first time, you should time how long it takes until the content is boiling.

Pea Stew

Put the peas into the kettle the evening before and soak them with plenty of water. The next day, bring the kettle with the peas to a boil and skim off the foam. It is very important that you always cook legumes without salt and only salt the soup when it is done, because the peas will otherwise foam a lot and, supposedly, will not cook. Cut the meat into bite-sized pieces and add after the soup comes to a boil the first time. Let it cook for one to one-and-a-half hours. Then add the peeled, diced potatoes and let them cook for half an hour.

Dice the bacon, onions, and vegetables. First render the bacon in a pan, then the onions; after that lightly braise the vegetables in the same pan. Put everything into the soup and let it cook for another half an hour. Season with pepper and salt. If you cannot obtain any flavor, then sugar and a bit of vinegar are missing. If you want to serve sausages with it, you should either heat these in a separate kettle or slice the sausages into bite-sized pieces and add them directly to the soup. They are easier to eat this way too, if you don't have a place to sit.

INGREDIENTS FOR 50 PERSONS

- 8 lbs (4kg) dried peas
- 8 lbs (4kg) pork (shoulder)
- 7 lbs (3kg) potatoes
- 1lb (500g) onions
- 1lb (500g) celery
- 1lb (500g) leeks
- 1lb (500g) bacon
- salt and pepper
- 2 teaspoons majoram
- 3 gal (15 l) water
- sugar
- a bit of vinegar

For soups, it is always difficult to accurately measure the amount of salt, but with 1 tablespoon per quart, you are on the right track. Weigh the needed salt and first add half of it, then again half of what you have left, and so forth. You can always add salt, but it is difficult to remove it!

Pea soup is the classic dish for campfire kitchens and can be easily stretched if more guests arrive.

Simply add sausage water to it until it has the consistency of instant mashed potatoes.

The ladle handle should be long enough so that it doesn't slide into the kettle.

Pea soup warms your body and soul.

Brown the meat by servings.

With the lid on let it simmer for some time.

Goulash Soup

INGREDIENTS FOR 50 PERSONS

- 10 lbs (5kg) beef
- 8 lbs (4kg) peeled potatoes
- 6 lbs (3kg) onions
- 10 red bell peppers
- 2 large cans tomato paste
- 5 large cans peeled tomatoes
- salt, pepper, paprika powder to taste
- 2 cups oil
- 3 gallons (12 l) water
- sauce thickener

Heat the oil in the pot, then brown the bite-sized meat pieces by servings and remove them from the pot. Brown the diced onions. Add the tomatoes and tomato paste. Add the water and bring it to a boil. Add the meat, season with paprika powder, and let it cook for one-and-a-half hours.

Add the diced potatoes and let it cook another half an hour. Add the diced bell peppers and bring it to a boil, then season to taste.

Finally produce a thick consistency using sauce thickener and season to taste.

You can also cook the goulash soup with twice the amount of meat and omit the potatoes. Then you have a proper goulash. In another kettle cook macaroni and now you have a super meal for kids.

A goulash soup that is worth seeing

Szegedine Goulash

- 2 lbs (1kg) goulash meat (half beef, half pork)
- 1/2 lb (250g) diced bacon
- 1 lb (500g) mushrooms
- 1 can peeled tomatoes (450 ml)
- 1 large can sauerkraut
- 5 onions, coarsely diced
- 1 red bell pepper, cut
- 1 bottle dry red wine
- 1 teaspoon each thyme, caraway, marjoram, ground pepper
- 2 teaspoons fine sweet paprika powder
- 1 teaspoon salt
- clarified butter for browning

Szegedine goulash is easy to prepare but thrills with its taste.

Thoroughly brown the meat on all sides in a pan, add the spices, and put the meat in the kettle. Brown the diced bacon, the onions, and the mushrooms until they are translucent, then put them in the kettle with the meat. Brown the bell pepper pieces and deglaze the pan with red wine. Put the whole thing into the kettle. Using fresh, clarified butter, brown the drained sauerkraut and put it in the kettle. Finally, add the peeled tomatoes with their liquid, fill it up with an additional two quarts of water or, better yet, broth, and let it simmer for two hours.

Season the goulash with pepper and salt at the end.

Szegedine Goulash is eaten as the main dish, without side dishes.

Brown the ingredients in order and add them to the kettle.

Then let the goulash simmer until the meat is tender.

Asado—Barbecuing like the Gauchos

If Argentinia is known for something, it is for its meat. The gauchos and their descendants consume it in giant quantities using a special barbecuing method called "asado." Even though asado actually just means "barbecuing," it is more than that. It stands for the whole event, for gathering with friends and a cozy evening with good meat and good red wine. The difference from grilling in America lies in the fact that in Argentina large portions of meat are cooked slowly and that you are already full when you are invited to asado. The guests arrive around noon and have eaten. Then they participate in the barbecuing and talk, and when the meat is done after a few hours, you eat together in the evening. Asado is approached with a lot more calm and relaxation than the hectic grilling here.

This method of grilling was actually born out of necessity, because the gauchos slaughtered one of the cattle from their herd in the evening and cooked it slowly by the fire. Originally they only had a few pieces of wood available, so it could not be spared to support the meat over the fire, so they came to place it next to the fire.Today, metal asado crosses are used.

The fire that is the basis for this cooking method is not exactly small. It is made with dry hardwood about as thick as your arm. A wheelbarrow of wood is just the right amount, for starters. Since erected crosses are hard to move, the fire is moved to the cross with a shovel if necessary.

Have extra wide aluminum foil ready in case it starts to rain. Then you simply protect the back side of the animals from cooling off with a layer of aluminum foil.

The closer the items to be grilled are to the embers, the hotter they will get. It is important to consider the wind first. The wind should blow from the items to be grilled to the fire so that it is only subject to little smoke. The meat cooks in the radiating heat, not the flames or the smoke. You should also take to heart the rule that you achieve the best results with slow cooking at relatively low temperatures. If you place your hand in front of the items to be grilled and can count to five slowly before having to withdraw it, you have the proper temperature. For beef ribs you only need to turn them once; you first grill the side with the ribs and then the other. Whether you also rotate the ribs so that the upper part ends up on the bottom or the other way around depends on how this part is cooking. For long pieces it will become necessary; for smaller pieces that are close to the fire anyhow, you can skip it.

You barbecue a suckling pig with the head up and the ribs to the fire to start with. This way the legs, the thickest pieces, receive the greatest heat. Then turn the piece with the head down,

Asado, as it should be: The meat is so tender
that it falls off the bones.

so the shoulder and neck cook too. At the end you can place the pork with the rind facing down horizontally onto two low blocks directly over the embers to crisp the rind. This only takes a few seconds, though.

An important utensil when barbecuing with this method is a meat thermometer. With it you can determine the core temperature of the meat. At 132° F (56° C), beef is medium done; above 160° F (70° C) it is gray and done. Pork, however, should definitely reach this higher core temperature. Don't fool yourself regarding the required time, because several hours are certainly required for this. For such a chunk of beef ribs six hours are the norm, for a suckling pig weighing 24 lbs (12kg), three hours are sufficient.

What can you barbecue? Simple answer: everything that fits on a spit. The typical piece is a "beef short rib," the side of the cattle with the ribs and the stomach paunch. The piece generally weighs about 26 to 30 lbs (13 to 15 kg), so it is not suitable for the cozy evening for two. The effort is only worth it when there are several people. Due to the large ribs, count on 1-1/2 lbs (750g) of uncooked meat per person. You have to pre-order this meat so you get the short ribs whole and not cut into pieces.

As another alternative for asado, suckling pig or whole lambs work. I would stop at a suckling pig weighing 24 to 30 lbs (12 to 15kg); with more weight the meat portions vary too much and are too thick to cook uniformly. The same applies to lambs. For boars, you should arrive at a weight of 24 lbs (12kg) without the rind and the head. Removing the rind is necessary; you can cut off the head. As with lamb you should brush boar with saltwater occasionally. A crisp rind, like that of the domestic pig, is not possible due to its natural anatomy.

The animal is placed onto the cross on its back on a large table. With an axe, remove the ribs along the spine so that the whole piece lies flat. With baling wire attach the piece to the cross bars by the legs. For suckling pigs the snout should also be secured with wire. Two or three additional wires that hold the spine to the bar are also necessary. For this task, you should keep in mind that the meat and the bones still hold together fairly well when raw, but this is not true once the meat cooks and the pork falls apart when it's done. You should also tighten everything now as tightly as possible since it is almost impossible once the spit is setup.

You have to cut a cross pattern into the rind of a suckling pig so it gets nice and crispy. Additionally, it contracts during cooking, so, if it weren't scored, entire plates would fall off the rind. With lamb you have to brush the meat so it doesn't dry out too much. For this use a glass of olive oil, in which you should squeeze a lemon and two to three pressed garlic cloves.

Spices? The easy part of asado is the seasoning: just rub it with a coarse sea salt and that's it! Whatever sticks to it, sticks to it. Due to the coarse crystals not as much salt sticks as would be the case with finer salt, and thus the meat is not too salty later on. The large chunks of salt loosen during the barbecuing. While eating you sprinkle additional coarse pepper onto the pieces.

Cut into thin slices across the fibers. Even a piece of beef rib—really only useful as soup meat—turns into a delicious meal, though, unfortunately, only after several hours. Don't approach this with the expectation of a "filet steak" either, because, even after hours, it is still quite firm to the bite.

It is important to properly attach the piece of meat or animal to the asado cross since you can hardly "correct" during the barbecuing.

Building an Asado Cross

An asado cross can be made by welding the elements together, but, of course, that is not possible for every reader. So we developed a frame that can easily be put together using parts available at the home improvement store. Taken apart, it fits into the trunk of a car and, when assembled, it can hold a weight of about 35 pounds (15kg).

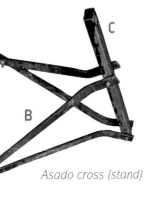

Asado cross (stand)

It consists of two parts, the cross and a stand. To build the asado cross requires only a hacksaw, a file for deflashing, and a drill with a 1/4-inch metal drill bit. The whole set-up is screwed together with 1/4-inch screws or 1/4-inch threaded rods and nuts, using the 1/4-inch drill bit to make the holes. The cross itself is built on a six-foot piece of 1-1/4" x 1/4" steel bar, in which two holes are drilled at 20 inches from each end to align with holes drilled in the crossbars. These are to hold the two crossbars. The crossbars also should be of 1-1/4" x 1/4" steel bar and about 2 feet wide, with two holes driled in the middle to align with those in the center support.

The stand is built around a length of steel rectangular tubing. Labeled part "C" in the illustration, it is 20 inches long with dimensions of 1-1/2" x 1/2" x 16-gauge. The support rod of the cross will fit inside of this. If your local home supply store does not have this, you can order it online. The pipe is drilled in two places to accept the braces and legs, once near the bottom end, and once about 10" up. In the illustration you can see how the stand is screwed together.

In the illustration, part "A" is a flat steel bar, 1-1/4" x 1/4" x 40", with a hole near the end and one at 20".

The brace, part "B" in the illustration, is of the same steel bar and is 20" long, with holes drilled near both ends.

The two bends on the parts A and B are done in a vice about three inches from the drilled end and angled by eye. The goal is to set the legs so that their ends are about 40 inches apart when opened. This will give a secure stand, even with the cross inserted. If they don't quite fit, some irregularities can be balanced out with the screws.

ASADO CROSS

• steel bar, 1-1/4" x 1/4" x 72" (drill holes at 20 inches from both ends)
• 2 steel bars, 1-1/4" x 1/4" x 2 feet (drill holes exactly in the middle to align with center post)

ASADO CROSS STAND

• rectangular pipe, 1-1/2" x 1/2" x 16-gauge x 20" long (drill holes near the end and at 10 inches up)
• 2 steel bars, 1-1/4" x 1/4" x 40" (drill holes near the end and at 20")
• 2 steel bars, 1-1/4" x 1/4" x 20" (a drill hole near each end)
• 1/4" screws or 1/4" threaded with enough nuts and washers

Side Dishes for Asado

INGREDIENTS

- 1 bulb garlic (four cloves are enough, too)
- 1 cup smooth parsley
- 1 cup fresh oregano leaves, alternatively 2 tablespoons dry oregano
- 2 teaspoons chili flakes
- 1/4 cup red wine vinegar
- 1/2 cup high quality olive oil
- 1 cup salt water

Chimichurri

Chimichurri is a spice sauce that is common in all of Argentina and the other South American states and is particularly served with beef and lamb. There are a lot of recipes for this but the most traditional one is certainly also the easiest.

Fresh and high-quality ingredients are decisive for the quality of the product. The basis is always saltwater, olive oil, vinegar, garlic, parsley, and oregano.

Mix the finely chopped garlic with the parsley (also finely chopped), the chili flakes, and the oregano. Stir in the olive oil and the vinegar and, at the end, the cup of saltwater, (see p. 154).

Chimichurri is best prepared the day before so the flavors can develop. This sauce will last for up to three weeks in the refrigerator.

Due to the ribs that were sawed earlier the piece is easily cut into servings.

The piece is thoroughly cooked.

Beef Ribs

For the beef ribs, you should buy a well-hung piece. For this it is necessary to inform your butcher in time since a side of beef short ribs is not always available. If the butcher still does his own slaughtering, then he can control it, but if he has to order the product, then it can go wrong. The piece weighs about 30 lbs (15 kg).

Saw through the ribs—but only the ribs, then you can better cut servings later on.

The meat is only spiced with coarse sea salt.

> **Tip:**
>
> **Pay attention to the direction of the wind when setting up the asado cross: The smoke should not head toward the meat.**

A nice piece of beef ribs.

Put it by the fire with the bones facing it.

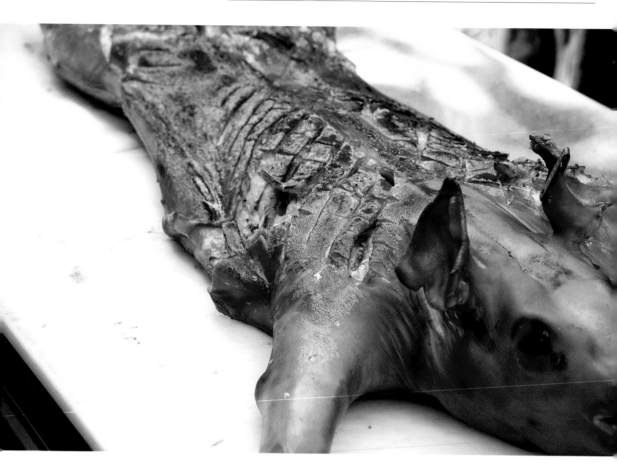

Suckling Pig

Be sure to attach the piece so that it still holds even when the meat loses its connectivity due to the cooking process. Otherwise the meat will fall into the fire as soon as it is done.

A suckling pig weighing 25 to 30 lbs (12 to 14 kg) is optimal for the asado grill. Purchase a suckling pig already frozen and thaw it. Then cut a diamond pattern about as thick as a finger into the rind with an extremely sharp knife, but only into the rind, not into the meat. During barbecuing the rind contracts and tears anyhow, and if you do not score the rind, it will fall into the fire in large chunks. On the inside, separate the ribs from the spine and open them up. This way you can attach the suckling pig to the bottom brace using the tendons of the hind legs.

As a backup, also attach it using several loops of bailing wire. Pull the suckling pig as hard as you can to the front by its front legs and attach these to the upper brace. Attach the head with a wire through the snout, and on the back use another two wires that you poke through the back, to the left and right of the spine, and twist behind the cross. Here, an iron bar with a filed notch helps to push the wire through a premade hole.

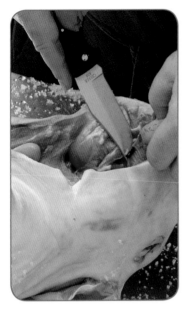

Cut out the tongue and the kidneys.

Separate the ribs from the spine.

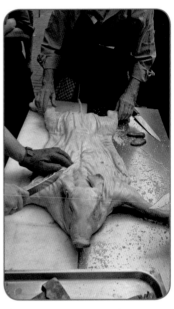

Score the rind crosswise.

Attach the piece with its back on the cross.

The suckling pig cooks first with its head facing up and the inside of the body toward the fire.

Here a view of the construction as seen from the back.

Use simple flower wire only, not the galvanized kind. When removing it from the cross, twist the wire open again. If you cut the wire with pliers, short pieces of wire could get into the food and hurt your guests.

Once the piece is attached to the cross, rub it well with coarse salt.

The cooking process is slightly different for a suckling pig than for a lamb. First, you have to bring the meat to a core temperature of at least 160° F (70° C). This works best with the head up and the inside of the body facing the fire. Support the legs with a shovel of embers below the legs; do the same with the blades and the neck when you turn the piece after two hours to have its head down and the inside of the body facing the fire. After two to three hours, the pork should be about done. Then you turn the pork with the rind toward the fire. After another hour, this side should be done too, but the rind is not quite crispy yet; that is left for the end. Turn the piece half an hour before serving with the inside toward the fire again, to reheat it.

To serve it, you just have to magically create a crispy crust. That is quite simple: Pull the embers apart with a shovel and with the help of another person hold the suckling pig very close to the embers. It only takes seconds before you hear the rind turning crisp. It pops like popcorn.

 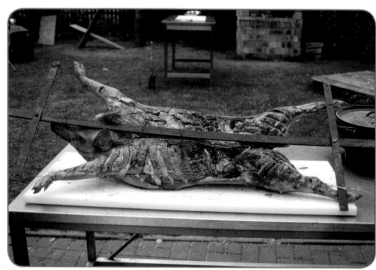

For crisping two people hold the asado cross with the suckling pig with the rind facing directly toward the embers.

Lamb

A lamb weighing 25-30 lbs (14kg) is just right. Lay the lamb on its back and open the legs and the rib cage. Then place an axe onto the rib attachments to the spine and hit the neck of the axe with your hand. This way you separate the ribs from the spine and can lay the animal down flat. Attach the lamb to the cross with wire. Since lamb is usually dry, you have to first moisten the meat with some water or salmuera (see next page), so the coarse salt will stick. Salt the animal and place it by the fire with the inside of the body facing the fire and the head up.

You don't need to worry that the meat will dry out. The silver skin on the meat will dry about one millimeter, then the meat will cook in its own juices underneath this parchment-like skin. During carving pull this skin off in large strips to get to a wonderfully juicy meat. After about three hours, you should rotate the meat, that is, with the back facing the fire; the head remains upright. Now it is time to heat the legs more by getting a shovel of embers from the fire and placing them under the legs.

You can also brush the lamb meat with a mixture of olive oil, lemon juice, and pressed garlic cloves.

Once the piece has some color on the inside, it is turned with the ribs facing outward.

The meat is already falling off the bones in the back area

You can completely cut the piece with a knife since all important bone connections have already been severed.

After another hour, rotate the piece with the head down and the back to the fire. Here, as well, support the blades by placing a shovel of fresh embers under them. After another hour, when the piece has been cooking for a total of five hours, turn it once again with the inside toward the fire and the legs facing down. Here you reheat the piece thoroughly one more time.

When cutting you should note that lamb easily tastes like old sheep if it doesn't reach the plate while hot. Therefore, gather your guests in time and let them participate in the final minutes by the fire and the cutting. The guests should also already have the accompaniments on their plate. It is better to have the guests waiting with their salad on the plate and then receiving their hot meat than for the meat to have to wait for the guests and cool off.

If you have properly barbecued the lamb then you merely have to remove it from the spit, pull off the parchment-like skin and divide the meat. The shoulder is so tender then that you can remove the meat from the bone with a spoon. Serve some chimichurri and a fresh baguette with it. You don't need more than that.

Chimichurri sauce tastes wonderful with lamb. You can find the recipe on page 148.

The leg is cooked through to the bone.

SALMUERA

Salmuera is saltwater that is used for asado as well as to sprinkle the lamb. Making it is as easy as can be: bBring one cup of water to a boil in a pot or a water cooker, mix in at least one tablespoon sal,t and stir. Undissolved salt should remain on the cup bottom. After it cools off, decant the liquid.

Deer

Deer is the principal type of game sought by sportmen. With a clean shot, it works very well for asado. Treat deer just like lamb; when broken open it is comparable in size with its 25 to 35 pounds.

A deer on the asado cross.

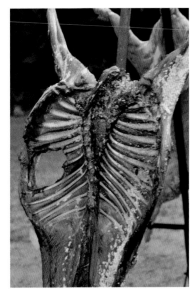

Cut away the bullet hole generously.

The ribs are dry but the legs, the back and the blades are wonderfully juicy.

Wild Boar

For wild boar an open weight of 35 lbs is just right for asado. However, the piece should have a clean shot. The skin is removed from the boar. Then it is rubbed with coarse salt and attached to the cross. You should cook it just as described for lamb (see page 153). Due to the removal of the skin, you do not get a crust with boar; scalding and depilating, as with a domestic pig, is not possible.

This young boar is supposed to turn into asado.

On the asado cross it cooks in the heat radiating from the fire.

A good roast even if young boar with its head still attached always looks like a pterosaur.

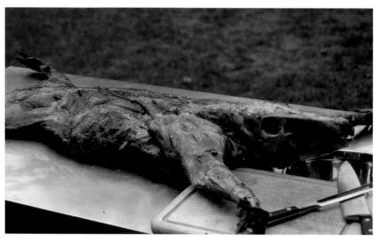

Entrecôte

For asado or rodizio—the Brazilian version of asado—you can also use more tender meat. Particularly well suited is marbled entrecôte or rib eye or prime rib. You should place this meat onto long skewers and cook it next to the fire or on low heat over the embers. It is also possible to cut the meat away on the outside and barbecue the next layer, but a lot of the delicious meat juice is lost this way.

Several skewers standing next to the fire with the best entrecôte steaks.

Duck

If you want to cook duck, then you should open it up as you do with lamb or other pieces. For this, cut the backbone out and press the bird flat. Cooking next to the fire, you can barbecue with the duck threaded on a branch or suspended on a rope as we showed earlier (see page 62).

Poke the branch fork through the duck.

The duck is cooking next to the fire.

With a bit of effort the duck will be crispy.

REAL BARBECUE

A smoker—heated properly—produces no more smoke than a cigarette, so it can even be used in developed areas.

General Remarks

In the American Southern states the slaves were allocated slaughter waste on the cotton plantations. Common were spareribs and brisket, the toughest part of a cattle's chest. They found a way to create delicious ways to use even these ingredients. To render this meat palatable—at least chewable—it needed to be cooked for a long time at low temperatures. This is how the "low and slow" of barbecuing (BBQ) developed.

By now, barbecuing is a household name, particularly in America, and stands not only for a type of preparation but also for celebrations and garden parties at which you grill. For a real barbecue you need a "smoker," in which you no longer just prepare spareribs and tough pieces of meat, but anything you can imagine, from the best roasts to steaks.

The Smoker at a Large Celebration

Like no other grilling device, a smoker lends itself to feeding a lot of people. In the cooking chamber of a large smoker, you can accommodate and simultaneously cook a 40-pound pork neck roast without a problem, which is enough for about 60 people. When preparing for a celebration, first preheat the smoker. Then you can prepare the rest—set up tables and chairs, prepare salads, set out beverages, etc. You can take care of the fire and check the temperature every 15 minutes.

Spareribs—but Properly!

An absolute must for every true BBQ party is ribs. I am not thinking of the cooked ribs in the vacuum-sealed package or the ribs marinated by the uninitiated butcher that are then cooked briefly on a hot grill. That turns the meat tough and half of the meat sticks stringy between your teeth and the other half still sticks to the bones. To prepare dreamy, tender ribs a smoker is ideal.

A fire is started in the fire box and soon you will be able to put the meat into the cooking chamber. Don't forget: Keep adding wood!

Where Does the Meat Come From?

For ribs there are two cuts, one are the rib cutlets that are bent more and were cut off directly from the spine; these are commonly called baby back ribs. Then there are the belly ribs that are adjacent to them and have grown together with cartilage at the sternum. These belly ribs are only slightly bent; the slab of ribs is a bit wider and slightly tapered.

As a main meal, with coleslaw, count on one slab of ribs per person; as finger food less will suffice.

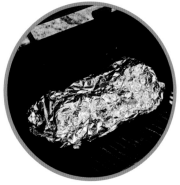

*The ribs cook for at least
two hours in aluminum foil.*

Prepare properly

On the inside of the ribs there is a very tough, thin skin that has to be removed before cooking. This does two things: it allows the spices to penetrate properly and makes the ribs much easier to eat. Removal is very easy: Loosen the skin at a rib with a small sharp knife and get a hold of the corner with a kitchen towel; you can then pull off the skin as a whole.

To end up with the ribs tender to the point of the bones letting themselves be turned out of the meat, you need time. The safest method is in the smoker according to the formula "3-2-1": The first three hours, the ribs are "smoked" at 230–250° F (110–120° C). Then they are placed into an aluminum foil packet with a shot of liquid (preferably the marinade in which the ribs were previously marinated) for two hours. Finally, the ribs are glazed at a slightly higher temperature for one hour. For this, brush the ribs with a sugar-sweetened marinade, let it dry on, then raise the temperature to 360° F (180° C) for a few minutes at the end, so the sugar part caramelizes and the ribs turn nice and dark.

Pork Neck from the Smoker

You should count on at least 10 ounces (300 grams) meat (raw weight) per person. You are always set with this. When smoking you cannot "add more" if you notice that there is not enough meat. Since pork neck is relatively inexpensive, you shouldn't skimp on the meat. If you invite 100 people and buy meat for an extra 10 people, then we are talking a small added cost of 10 dollars at most. If you have to be concerned about $10 when making your calculations, you should stay away from such an event, because the beverages will run a multiple of those costs.

For a celebration with about 100 people you can plan as follows: Into the large cooking chamber of the smoker place a pork neck that is about 45 pounds (20 kg), which will easily feed 60 people at once. Don't worry if you have leftovers. You can enjoy the meat as cold cuts or freeze it. To empty the cooking chamber, remove the cooked roasts and keep them warm in an insulated chest (under no circumstance place it on a chafing dish; the roast will dry out). Then you can, for example, place the trout (or salmon slices or chicken breasts) into the cooking chamber; they only take half an hour, and you already have another 20 servings ready.

Season the neck roast (or inject the roast with a spice solution). Place the roast into the smoker let it cook at 250 to 260° F (120 to 130° C) for about six hours.

INGREDIENTS PER PERSON

- 10–14 oz (300–400g) meat, e.g. neck roast
- 1/2 to 1 baked potato with tsatsiki
- 1/4 trout (smoked hot)
- 2 oz (50g) baked beans
- Salad buffet
- 1/4 lb (100g) rib-eye steak

The temperature in the cooking chamber is not uniform everywhere, so the roasts have to
be repositioned occasionally.

Due to the hot smoke fumes the outer layer develops a crust and the roast cooks in its own juices. It is important to leave the roast alone. With a filled cooking chamber it is difficult to maintain 260° F (130° C) on the back thermometer and to prevent flames from entering the cooking chamber. It is best to line the first 12 inches (30cm) of the grate with aluminum foil so the meat doesn't burn there. Every two hours, rotate the roasts with those in the back moving to the front and vice versa. Under no circumstance poke the roast with a fork since it will lose a lot of meat juice that way. Turning is best done with heatproof gloves and a spatula. You should achieve a core temperature over 165° F (75° C) in your roasts. Then they aren't just done, but also tender and soft.

Trout

Trout do well in the 175° F (80° C) zone in the tower of the smoker. Serving-size fish (1/2–3/4 lb each [200–300 g]) are placed into a salt brine for two hours. The brine is very easy to make: Place one raw potato into the water and keep adding salt until the potato rises. After two hours in the brine, the fish are dried off and placed on the grates with their opened bellies. On the top two grates you can fit about ten trout each. This takes care of preparing twenty servings for the fish eaters. The trout can be smoked for four hours without worries. They are done when the back fin can be pulled out of the meat. They are usually cooked when the skin turns golden yellow. Since the skin turns leathery very quickly, it is not that easy to pull the back fin out. After four hours at 100° F (80° C), the trout are definitely done.

The smoker's tower has different temperature zones in which you can, for example, smoke trout or prepare baked potatoes.

Fixings

As a side dish, baked potatoes are simply a must. You should precook these and then pile them into the bottom of the tower. Since the potatoes are already done, they no longer need to sit in the hot zone, rather it is enough if they turn a bit leathery on the outside from the smoke and stay hot.

Baked beans or cowboy beans are also a delicious fixing. Especially if you are having a BBQ in cold weather, a warm side dish is better than a cold salad. About 1/4 cup (2 oz or 50g) Per person is enough, since not everyone will take some. For 100 people, ten to fifteen pounds (5–7kg) should be enough. Here, as well, you shouldn't be too stingy since leftover beans can easily be frozen in small portions and beans don't cost too much anyway.

Tip:

For a salad buffet, you are best off placing each salad ingredient into an individual bowl, that is, the green salad, the bell peppers, the onions etc., as well as the dressings and marinades. This has two advantages.: First, everyone can take what they like and omit what they don't like. Second, the salad ingredients have different shelf lives and this way when the first wilts, it doesn't spoil everything else. Bell peppers last in the refrigerator for a few days even cut. Because they have no dressing, the salad ingredients also can be used on other things, like soups or pizza toppings.

Spice immediately before cooking with only sea salt and pepper.

Entrecôte Steak: The Tasty Tidbit at the end

To turn the event into a real highlight, you should prepare the right steaks. I always use beef entrecôte steaks that I cut the thickness of two finger widths. I first brown them in the fire chamber over plenty of embers on a cast iron grill grate, so they get a nice burn pattern. Then I let the steaks cook in the cooking chamber up to the desired temperature. I cut these large steaks into slices because if you hand out the steaks (each nearly 1 pound) as a whole, too much remains on the plates—pure waste.

The steaks are served at the end for two reasons: First, people are not as hungry, so there is less demand, and the steaks can really be prepared individually. Second, the guests savor the steak because the first ravenous appetite has already been quenched, so that less is needed of the expensive beef.

Allow 1/4 pound (100g) per person

You can purchase these cuts vacuum sealed at wholesale. You should store this meat as a "reserve" in the refrigerator. You only cut open the package if you really need the meat. If there are leftovers, then, in the best case scenario, it is in the unopened package, in which it will last for a few more days. With this reserve, you feed the last insatiable few and, if something is not eaten, then it is not the typical leftover, but meat of the best quality.

Pure BBQ!. Steffen Eichhorn, Stefan Marquard, & Stephan Otto. Powerhouse German foodies Steffen Eichhorn, Stefan Marquard, and Stephan Otto tackle grilling and smoking everything from oysters to mini beer keg suckling pigs. Through many hours spent BBQing and tasting, the trio has developed 34 excellent recipes including pierced perch, melon and halibut skewers, beech plank salmon, and antipasti, as well as classics for the smoker—pulled pork and beef brisket.
Size: 8 1/2" x 11" • 47 color photos • 128 pp.
ISBN: 978-0-7643-4013-0 • hard cover • $24.99

Dutch Oven: Cast-Iron Cooking Over an Open Fire. Carsten Bothe. The Dutch oven has been popular on the grill and barbecue scene, and cooking with the "black pots" over an open fire has become a fashionable cult. Now you can learn to conjure such dishes as juicy roasts, hearty casseroles, or baked crisp bread. Desserts, bean dishes, or casseroles, become child's play through simple directions making cooking easy and fun, even for a beginner.
Size: 7" x 10" • 147 color images • 176 pp.
ISBN: 978-0-7643-4218-9 • soft cover • $29.99

The Perfect Sausage: Making and Preparing Homemade Sausage. Karsten "Ted" Aschenbrandt. Join BBQ master Karsten "Ted" Aschenbrandt as he demonstrates how to make the perfect sausage. From raw ingredients to kitchen gear and gadgets to secret tips for better flavor, this cookbook covers everything you need to know in easy illustrated steps. Nearly 30 different sausage styles from around the globe and 26 recipes featuring sausage are included.
Size: 8 1/8" x 9 1/8" • 88 color images • 120 pp.
ISBN: 978-0-7643-4302-5 • soft cover • $19.99

Grilling Like a Champion. Rudolf Jaeger. Learn how to impress friends and family by perfecting their favorite cuisine, and find out how to win grilling competitions. Professional grill masters share some of the best-kept secrets of the trade, including information on purchasing the most reliable equipment, using the right type of grill and fueling method, and shopping for the freshest ingredients.
Size: 8 1/8" x 9 1/8" • 396 color photos • 232 pp.
ISBN: 978-0-7643-4498-5 • hard cover • $34.99

Schiffer books may be ordered from your local bookstore, or they may be ordered directly from the publisher by writing to:

Schiffer Publishing, Ltd. • 4880 Lower Valley Rd. • Atglen, PA 19310
(610) 593-1777; Fax (610) 593-2002 • E-mail: Info@schifferbooks.com

Please visit our website catalog at *www.schifferbooks.com*
or write for a free catalog.

Printed in China